SSR Paper 19

The Security Sector Governance–Migration Nexus: Rethinking how Security Sector Governance matters for migrants' rights

DCAF-Commissioned SSR Policy Paper

Sarah Wolff

]u[
ubiquity press
London

DCAF Geneva Centre for Security Sector Governance
DCAF
Geneva

Published by
Ubiquity Press Ltd.
Unit 322–323
Whitechapel Technology Centre
75 Whitechapel Road
London E1 1DU
www.ubiquitypress.com

First published 2021

Cover image: "Immigration Officer processing Travel Documents" Robert Beechey 2012 © International Organization for Migration. All rights reserved. Image used in this publication under Fair Use permissions. https://medialib.iom.int/preview/3562

Print and digital versions typeset by Siliconchips Services Ltd.

ISBN (Paperback): 978-1-911529-92-7
ISBN (PDF): 978-1-911529-93-4
ISBN (EPUB): 978-1-911529-94-1
ISBN (Mobi): 978-1-911529-95-8

Series: SSR Papers
ISSN (Print): 2571-9289
ISSN (Online): 2571-9297

DOI: https://doi.org/10.5334/bcl

The full text of this book has been peer-reviewed to ensure high academic standards. For full review policies, see http://www.ubiquitypress.com/

Suggested citation:
Wolff, S. 2021. *The Security Sector Governance–Migration Nexus: Rethinking how Security Sector Governance matters for migrants' rights*. London: Ubiquity Press. DOI: https://doi.org/10.5334/bcl. License: CC-BY-NC

To read the free, open access version of this book online, visit https://doi.org/10.5334/bcl or scan this QR code with your mobile device:

Table of Contents

Chapter 6: Conclusions and Policy Recommendations 51

References 57

List of Figures, Boxes and Tables

Figures

Boxes

Tables

SSR Papers

The DCAF SSR Papers provide original, innovative and provocative analysis on the challenges of security sector governance and reform. Combining theoretical insight with detailed empirically-driven explorations of state-of-the-art themes, SSR Papers bridge conceptual and pragmatic concerns. Authored, edited and peer reviewed by SSR experts, the series provides a unique platform for in-depth discussion of a governance-driven reform agenda, addressing the overlapping interests of researchers, policy-makers and practitioners in the fields of development, peace and security.

DCAF, the Geneva Centre for Security Sector Governance, is dedicated to making states and people safer. Good security sector governance, based on the rule of law and respect for human rights, is the very basis of development and security. DCAF assists partner states in developing laws, institutions, policies and practices to improve the governance of their security sector through inclusive and participatory reforms based on international norms and good practices.

About the Author

Sarah Wolff is the Director of the Centre for European Research and Reader (Associate Professor) at Queen Mary University of London. Since 2019, she is Principal Investigator for the Jean Monnet Centre of Excellence NEXTEUK project on the future of EU-UK Relations. She is Visiting Professor at the College of Europe and a Senior Research Associate at the Netherlands Institute of International Relations (Clingendael). In 2021 she was elected Commitee member of the University Association for Contemporary European Studies (UACES). A leading scholar of European integration, she has recently co-edited a special issue for the *Journal of European Integration* on EU responses to the Covid-19 Pandemic. A work on migration has included research on Frontex, the role of cities in managing migration in Morocco, the EU-Readmission Agreement negotiations with Morocco and Turkey and extensive consultancy work on EU related migration issues. Dr Wolff is an expert of European migration and border management policies, EU foreign policy and democratization efforts, as well as EU-Arab Mediterranean relations and EU-Islam relations. She is Editor of the journal *Mediterranean Politics*. Her manuscript with Michigan University Press on 'Secular Power Europe and Islam: Identity and foreign policy'(summer 2021) is the result of data collected through a Fulbright-Schuman and a Leverhulme research grant. Her monograph 'The Mediterranean Dimension of the European Union's Internal Security' (Palgrave, 2012) was one of the first comprehensive studies exploring the externalisation of EU Justice and Home Affairs policy to North Africa and the Middle East. She received the LISBOA Research Award 2012 for her book 'Freedom, Security and Justice after Lisbon and Stockholm' (Asser, 2012; co-edited). Before joining academia, Dr Wolff worked at the European Commission and the European Parliament.

Declaration

Executive Summary

This paper argues that there is a need to improve linkages between security sector governance/reform (SSG/R) and migration. Going beyond the state-centric understanding of security sector reform (SSR), it provides a comprehensive view of the relationship between SSG/R and migration and makes a series of practical recommendations to operationalize a better inclusion of migration issues at domestic, regional and international levels of SSG/R. It provides guidance as to how the military, police forces, intelligence services, border security services, judicial institutions, interior ministries, private actors, civil society organizations and parliaments should rethink the inclusion of migrants' rights at the heart of their professional practice.

Migration is a transnational policy issue, with flows that challenge artificially politicized categories of who a migrant is and classifications around countries of origin, transit and destination. This transnational nature calls for a decentring and recentring of our understanding and conceptualization of the relationship between migration and SSG/R. So far the SSG/R–migration nexus has been overlooked, owing to, first, the state-centric nature of SSG/R, which tends to treat SSG/R mostly within the national context. Second, this state-centric focus has also led migration to be treated mostly as a security threat that suffers from the turf wars between internal and external security actors (Wolff, 2017). Third, SSG/R is a concept coined in the 1990s that needs to be revamped in the light of a fast-changing environment. The Covid-19 pandemic is likely to have an important impact on migrants' remittances, as well as to intensify the racialized and gendered implications that had already been visible with globalisation and labour migrants' recruitment throughout the world (Anderson and Anderson, 2000). There is a general rise of prejudices towards racial and ethnic minorities and the pandemic of 2020 has constrained mobility while increasing migrants' and refugees' vulnerability. Migrants still continue to cross the Mediterranean, though, and Channel crossings have not stopped. The COVID-19 crisis has also offered an opportunity to think again about the essential work of migrants in key areas of economies all over the world, mostly as frontline workers in the farming industry, transport or the health sector.

A successful reconceptualization of SSG/R in relation to migration involves a decentring approach that should help to evolve from an institutional approach and instead broaden our understanding to 'meanings produced (i.e. meanings around the term "migrant"), to narratives constructed (i.e. the migration crisis) as well as the practices it entails', i.e. such as SSG/R practices. The challenge is thus to recentre the SSG/R focus on migrants' and refugees' rights and safety as a co-creation of state security (and not the reverse). The added value is thus to induce creative thinking beyond the 'safe, orderly and regular migration' dominant policy narrative that 'tends to unilaterally privilege the wishes and needs of receiving country governments (and employers or other stakeholders) disregarding the country of origin, country of transit and own migrant perspective' (Mouthaan, 2019, Collett and Ahad, 2017, quoted in Triandafyllidou, 2020). Following the adoption of the Global Compacts on Migration and on Refugees, this paper argues that SSG/R, defined as the 'formal and informal influences of all structures, institutions and actors involved in security provision, management and oversight at national and local levels',[1] should decentre from the national narrow understanding of security sector and instead recentre its reflection on taking into account the views of countries of origin and transit, as well as that of migrants. Ultimately, this shift will lead to improving migrants' and refugees' rights at various levels of governance: global, regional and local.

The main argument is that improving migrants' rights and conceptual linkages between SSG/R and migration is best achieved, by decentring our gaze, namely going beyond the 'national' and 'state-centric' view that characterizes traditionally SSG/R and to consider the agency of both migrants and SSG/R actors. First from a migrants' perspective, it is key for SSG/R actors to go beyond traditional legal classifications and to consider the diversity of personal situations that involve refugees, stranded migrants and asylum seekers, which might endorse different roles at different times of their journeys and lives. Second, the transnational nature of migration calls for a transnationalization of SSG/R too. For too long the concept has mostly been applied within the national setting of SSG/R institutions and actors. Migration calls for a clear decentring that involves a transnational dimension and more work among transnational actors and policymakers to facilitate a norm transfer from the domestic to the interstate and international level. As such, the 'transnational' nature of migration and its governance needs to be 'domesticated' within the national context in order to change the mindset of SSG/R actors and institutions.[2]

More importantly, the paper argues that poor SSG/R at home produces refugees and incentivizes migrants to leave their countries after being victims of violence by law enforcement and security services. During migrants' complex and fragmented journeys, good security sector governance is fundamental to address key challenges faced by these vulnerable groups. I also argue that a better understanding of migrants' and refugees' security needs is beneficial and central to the good governance of the security sector.

Dr Sarah Wolff
Queen Mary University of London
s.wolff@qmul.ac.uk
17 February 2021

---

[1] DCAF (n.d.) Security Sector Governance, SSR Backgrounder. https://www.dcaf.ch/sites/default/files/publications/documents/DCAF_BG_1_Security_Sector_Governance_EN.pdf.

[2] I am grateful to Manea Gabriela for this suggestion.

Abbreviations

EBCG	European Border and Coast Guard
EU	European Union
IDPs	Internally displaced people
IMF	International Monetary Fund
IOM	International Organization for Migration, also known as the UN Agency for Migration
JHA	Justice and home affairs
GAMM	Global Approach to Migration and Mobility
GCM	Global Compact for Migration
OECD	Organisation for Economic Co-operation and Development
OHCHR	Office of the United Nations High Commissioner for Human Rights
OSCE	Organization for Security and Co-operation in Europe
UNHCR	Office of the United Nations High Commissioner for Human Rights
SSG	Security Sector Governance
SSG/R	Security Sector Governance and Reform
SSR	Security Sector Reform

CHAPTER 1

Introduction

COVID-19 has not only revealed how weak globalized healthcare systems are, and how diversely countries have reacted to the crisis, but most certainly it has also exposed the most marginalized populations to greater vulnerability. Among these, migrants, asylum seekers and refugees are the most affected. First, given the looming economic crisis for migrants and their families, it is likely that remittances will be affected. The closing down of borders and lockdown measures have importantly affected the mobility of labour migration and many seasonal workers were not able to go to work in 2020. Others, like migrant workers from Eastern Europe, were among the few Europeans to travel by charter plane to other European countries to harvest strawberries and asparagus (Weisskircher, Rone, Mendes, 2020). Healthcare systems in several countries also depend on foreign doctors and nurses, and many agree that the recognition of the skills of foreign refugee doctors would be incredibly useful for systems such as the National Health Service (NHS) in the UK (Taylor, 2020). Suddenly there is a realization that migrants' skills are useful to economies.

Like in the migration governance crisis experienced in 2015, COVID-19 has revealed the acute difficulties of an international governance system that prioritizes states' interests over migrants' and the risks of a lack of a coordinated answer in Europe and worldwide, and more specifically destination countries' interest over those of the countries of origin and transition, and migrants themselves. Although the Global Compact for Safe, Orderly and Regular Migration (GCM), acclaimed in Marrakech in December 2018, which followed the 2016 UN New York Declaration for Refugees and Migrants, is a first attempt to foster increased international cooperation between countries of origin, transit and destination, as well as with civil society and private actors, the role of SSR actors and improved SSG in migration has not been systematically and comprehensively assessed. As this SSR paper goes to press a major actor in EU Security Sector Governance, Frontex, the European Border and Coast Guard Agency is being investigated by the EU Anti-Fraud Office (OLAF). Next to issues of fraud and contacts with unregistered lobbyists,

How to cite this book chapter:
Wolff, S. 2021. *The Security Sector Governance–Migration Nexus: Rethinking how Security Sector Governance matters for migrants' rights.* Pp. 1–3. London: Ubiquity Press. DOI: https://doi.org/10.5334/bcl.a. License: CC-BY-NC

there has been also accusations of pushbacks of migrants, leading Members of European Parliament (MEP) have denounced issues of accountability. This is a timely example supporting the argument that striving for better and ethically sound SSG/R is supportive of migrants' rights.

This paper considers for the first time the links between security sector governance (SSG) and migration. The paper argues that good SSG should be considered an integral part in improving migrants' and refugees' rights. Equally, it shows that better integration of migrants' and refugees' security needs, not only the national security of destination countries, as well as vulnerability assessments, is contributing to better SSG/R.

There is indeed little knowledge on the role that deficient SSG might have in fuelling migratory flows and refugees leaving their countries. SSG/R actors and institutions are interacting with migrants and refugees at various stages of their personal journeys. In order to ensure a safe, accountable, transparent, fair and efficient policy, good governance mechanisms are indispensable. Border guards, police officers, the judiciary and core power ministries such as interior ministries, but also the military, the intelligence services, private actors, civil society, independent oversight bodies and parliaments, all have a role to play in ensuring democratic oversight, the effectiveness of the security sector in relation to migration, principles of good governance and good service delivery.

This paper delivers the first ever comprehensive study on the SSG–migration nexus and makes policy recommendations on how SSG should better take migration into account. It is shown that efforts to improve SSG in origin, transit and destination countries can benefit migration policies as well as migrants' and refugees' rights and safety. Calling for a decentring approach, this paper calls for a full rethinking of the SSG/R–migration nexus, as described in Figure 1. It is about moving away from the state-centric lens and also the security interest of the predominant country of destination. In an ideal world where good SSG/R prevails, there is a guarantee that law enforcement officials are paid, that oversight and legitimacy prevail. Good SSG/R also means more interaction with local and community actors, which are fundamental to making sure that SSG is likely to play a protective role in migrants' journeys instead of being a driving factor. Although the drivers of migration are multiple, good SSG will prevent abuses towards refugees and internally displaced people, for instance. It would also ensure better justice for victims of traffickers. Good SSG would ensure that transnational borderlands are a bit safer for people crossing borders. Research has indeed shown that, when borderlands managed by the security sector are 'ungoverned', 'citizens may find shadow citizenship imposed by violent non-state groups more in line with, and responsive to, their everyday live needs than a social contract with an absent state' (Idler, 2018: 68).

This protective role of SSG ensures that the most vulnerable groups in society, such as refugees, internally displaced people and migrants, are protected. Taking a SSG approach in migration is also very innovative as it helps to shift the focus from thinking that improving the security sector is only the responsibility of the origin and transit countries. It helps to rebalance that view and shows that destination countries' SSG also plays a decisive role. The paper also makes the case for a dynamic understanding of the SSG–migration link that would shift the focus from a state-centrist approach to include an individual and community-based understanding as well as a better acknowledgement of migration as a transnational phenomenon. If state institutions are central to the delivery of SSG, the subnational and transnational levels of SSG should be better acknowledged.

After reviewing the key terms of migration and its drivers in chapter 2, chapter 3 outlines how SSG is part of the implementation of the GCM. SSR actors play a role in shaping migratory routes and refugees' incentives to leave, in explaining migrants' and refugees' resilience, in protecting migrants and refugees, and in providing security. Although it cautions against artificial classifications and the term of 'transit migration', chapter 4 reviews what the core challenges are in the countries of origin, transit and destination. Chapter 5 provides a detailed overview of the linkages between migration and each security actor: the military, police forces, intelligence services, border guards, interior ministries, private actors, criminal justice, parliaments, independent oversight bodies and civil society. Chapter 6 formulates some recommendations.

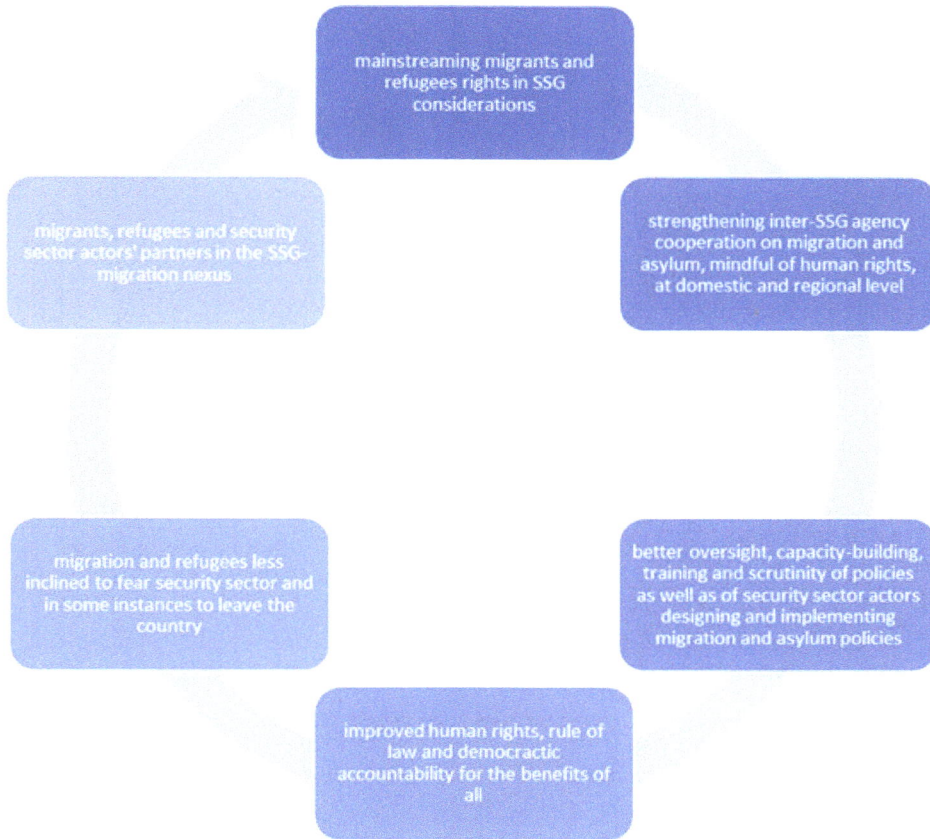

Figure 1: The virtuous cycle of the SSG/R–migration nexus.

This paper is the result of a qualitative methodology that has combined a focus group and expert interviews. The first step involved an expert roundtable hold on 24 October 2018 at DCAF in Geneva with experts from UNHCR, IOM and OHCHR, which enabled the key challenges of the study to be identified by engaging with key stakeholders. Then the study was deepened by desk research, and interviews with migration and SSG officials were held in March and April 2019.

CHAPTER 2

Migration: Trends and Terminology

Migration is a phenomenon that has accelerated with the expansion of globalization and subsequent rising social inequalities, the acceleration of climate change, and the desire to get better jobs and to support family members staying at home. This chapter provides some insights into the different types of situations that are often too easily aggregated under the term 'migrant' (2.1). Then it shows that the design and implementation of migration policies in various countries have overwhelmingly focused on the security and economic dimensions, contributing to shaping the nature and direction of migratory flows (2.2).

2.1 Who migrates and why?

In this paper we use the terms 'migrant' and 'refugee' to generically capture the wide diversity of people crossing borders for different reasons. The official definition of a migrant provided by IOM, the UN migration agency, is:

> any person who is moving or has moved across an international border or within a State away from his/her habitual place of residence, regardless of (1) the person's legal status; (2) whether the movement is voluntary or involuntary; (3) what the causes for the movement are; or (4) what the length of the stay is. (IOM, 2019)

This definition is rather broad and 'inclusivist' as it then considers that refugees can be considered migrants. This is at odds with the residualist view promoted by the UNHCR, which advocates for a definition that excludes refugees since they are more vulnerable and therefore should not fall under the definition of migrants (Carling, 2016).

These definitional debates in fact hide some tensions around the terminology, as indeed 'migrants' seems to be used and abused by policymakers and media to describe situations that

---

How to cite this book chapter:
Wolff, S. 2021. *The Security Sector Governance–Migration Nexus: Rethinking how Security Sector Governance matters for migrants' rights*. Pp. 5–9. London: Ubiquity Press. DOI: https://doi.org /10.5334/bcl.b. License: CC-BY-NC

are all very different. The term 'migrants' has become politically loaded and 'often conflates issues of immigration, race/ethnicity, and asylum' (Anderson and Blinder, 2017: 2). Indeed, in terms of data, 'migrants might be defined by foreign birth, by foreign citizenship, or by their movement into a new country to stay temporarily (sometimes for as little as a year) or to settle for the long-term' (Ibid: 2). Beyond the political implications for the treatment of migrants politically and in the media, definitions are also important from a legal point of view, in terms of attributing rights or not, as well as for determining datasets and thus policy decisions.

A common distinction is the one between 'regular' and 'irregular' migration, which has arisen from the criminalization of migrants over the past decades. These definitions are set by states, which after all decide who gets in or not to their territory: 'irregular migration is [thus] not an independent social phenomenon but exists in relation to state policies and is a social, political and legal construction' (Düvell, 2013: 276). Everyday realities show that these definitions may not always capture individual journeys of people experiencing very different situations: some people starting with a legal migration status might for instance end up their journey as irregular migrants. 'Refugees' refers to vulnerable people who are in need of protection and fleeing their countries. These refugees can obtain the status of asylum seeker or subsidiary protection, but they may also end up being considered irregular migrants by the country of origin and be returned. Also, new categories of displaced people have appeared, challenging conventional tools of international law. Next to the 'mixed migratory flows', the Arab uprisings have seen more 'stranded migrants'. These are migrants who are either in transit or at destination in North Africa, Yemen, Turkey and Greece but have no support from their governments (Chetail and Braeunlich, 2013). This was the case for workers from Vietnam, Thailand, Turkey, Ghana and Senegal who were left behind by their companies, lacking the means to get back home after the fall of the Qadhafi regime. State failure in Libya also meant that those who managed to return home, such as Egyptian migrants, returned to precarious conditions back in the Delta and Upper Nile, thus becoming potential candidates for crossing the Mediterranean (Marfleet and Hanieh, 2014).

Box 1: Migration: challenging definitions

Asylum seeker is defined as *'someone whose request for sanctuary has yet to be processed. Every year, around one million people seek asylum [worldwide]'* (UNHCR, 2019).

Internally displaced people *'stay within their own country and remain under the protection of its government, even if that government is the reason for their displacement. They often move to areas where it is difficult for us to deliver humanitarian assistance and as a result, these people are among the most vulnerable in the world'* (UNHCR, 2019).

Irregular migrants is a problematic definition that is contested since laws criminalize migrants in different ways. We therefore suggest considering the definitions of irregular foreign residents (IFR) and irregular foreign workers (IFW) instead. Clandestino defines them as follows:
'IFR are foreign nationals without any legal resident status in the country they are residing in, and persons violating the terms of their status so that their stay may be terminated'.
'IFW are foreign nationals working in the shadow economy, including those with a regular residence status who work without registration to avoid due taxes and regulations' (Clandestino, 2019).

Labour migration is the *'[m]ovement of persons from one State to another, or within their own country of residence, for the purpose of employment. Labour migration is addressed by* *most States in their migration laws. In addition, some States take an active role in regulating outward labour migration and seeking opportunities for their nationals abroad'* (IOM, 2019). This can include, depending on each country's regulation seasonal workers, low-skilled or high-skilled migrants.

Migrants are defined as *'any person who is moving or has moved across an international border or within a State away from his/her habitual place of residence, regardless of (1) the person's legal status; (2) whether the movement is voluntary or involuntary; (3) what the causes for the movement are; or (4) what the length of the stay is'* (IOM, 2019).

Refugees are protected by international law and the term is defined according to the 1951 Geneva Convention as any person who, *'owing to well-founded fear of being persecuted for reasons of race, religion, nationality, membership of a particular social group or political opinion, is outside the country of his nationality and is unable or, owing to such fear, is unwilling to avail himself of the protection of that country; or who, not having a nationality and being outside the country of his former habitual residence as a result of such events, is unable or, owing to such fear, is unwilling to return to it. In the case of a person who has more than one nationality, the term "the country of his nationality" shall mean each of the countries of which he is a national, and a person shall not be deemed to be lacking the protection of the country of his nationality if, without any valid reason based on well-founded fear, he has not availed himself of the protection of one of the countries of which he is a national'* (UNHCR, 1951).

Reasons to migrate involve fleeing poverty, conflict, environmental disasters and economic prospect. Getting a better job and better pay or sending money home via remittances are among the two main factors quoted by West Africans when asked 'what is the main reason you would migrate to another country?' (Kirwin and Anderson, 2018: 12). The decision to migrate is often linked to a collective choice in the community and not only to an individual decision. Thus, a study that surveyed families in Senegal and in Mali showed that often the 'extended family' or the village send people abroad 'with a strategic view': 'These people invest a sizable amount of resources for sending their most promising offspring to the city or even abroad', which is related to the remittances and productive potential (Azam and Gubert, 2006: 427). In 2018, remittances reached a record high of $529 billion, which was already an increase of 9.6% compared to 2017 (World Bank, 2019). COVID-19 will definitely impact the flow of remittances, but, as seen in the previous financial crisis, it is also possible that migrants even send higher amounts of money back home as a safety net for job loss in their country of origin.

State failure, conflict and war are strong motives for people to leave their home country. Accordingly, state failure 'begins … when a state cannot manage conflicts to minimize violence, ensure physical security, protect human rights, and provide essential services and development opportunities' (Deng, 2004: 16). State failure is often a reason for migration and leads to high numbers of internally displaced people (IDPs). Usually it corresponds to a high degree of human insecurity. Yet, because IDPs remain inside state borders, there is little consideration for how it might also create further reasons for IDPs to migrate.

The overly securitized framing of migration in the public debate has unfortunately led to overlook what social and economic factors drive migrants to leave their country, as well as whether corruption, the lack of rule of law and the lack of accountable SSG could actually be drivers of migration. The global discourse on migration overwhelmingly focuses on the interests of the countries of destination thus overlooks that migrants are trapped by state-driven definitions and that legal statuses also reflect the economic, security and political interests of countries of destination. For instance, there is no debate at present on the fact that the increased securitized border controls

---

Box 2: Data on migratory flows (UNHCR, 2019)

There were **272 million total estimated international migrants worldwide**, of whom 83.6 million were born in Asia, 82.3 million in Europe, 58.6 million in North America, 26.5 million in Africa, 11.6 million in Latin America and the Caribbean, and 8.9 million in Oceania.

In 2018, there were **37,000 displacements every day** and 'nearly 4 out of every 5 refugees lived in countries neighboring their countries of origin' (UNHCR, 2019: 2).

In total, **70.8 million people are 'forcibly displaced'** (UNHCR); this includes people coerced to move from their home, namely internally displaced people (IDPs) (41.3 million), refugees (25.9 million) and asylum seekers (3.5 million). In 2018 this reached the highest number known since the creation of the UNHCR.

---

throughout the world might be driven by state interest and a narrow understanding of national security. The global paradox of increased border controls in a mobile world nonetheless highlights a sharp contradiction. To what extent has poor security sector governance contributed to this trend? Is the practice of the security sector regarding border and migration control also affected? What form does it take and what impact does it have on migrants and refugees? Could an inclusion of migration into the objectives of SSG improve migrants' and refugees' rights?

2.2 The liberal paradox of state-centric policies

Decentring our understanding of migration governance, and in particular its relationship with SSG/R, requires asking SSG actors and institutions to be self-reflective about their security sector practice. This involves thinking differently about migration, as a transnational whole where SSG actors play an integral part. Although the state continues to play an important part, state-centrism is narrowly leading states to consider (1) migration to be an external threat to national security, and (2) that SSG/R is 'foreign' to migration. Instead, a self-reflective process on SSG/R should lead actors to rethink how state-centric and neo-liberal policies have fundamentally shaped migration flows as we know them.

First, a state-centric view has led to understand migration as a political risk for states (Hollifield, 2006: 886). Although borders were less significant in the past, they became more relevant in the inter-war period, with the rise of nationalism, and played a function in protecting markets. Since the Second World War, though, migration has mostly taken an economic function, responding to the liberal requirements of free trade: 'ensuring material wealth and power has required states to risk greater economic openness and to pursue policies of free trade' (Rosecrance, 1986, in Hollifield, 2006). Open migration regimes towards old colonies were key in the post-Second World War reconstruction period. Nowadays, migration has become a structural factor of world economies. In Europe and in North America, migrants 'take the dirty, dangerous and dull jobs that nationals do not want; they work in sectors where social protection or labor benefits are scarce' (Favell, 2014: 280). Workers, owing to the structure of the globalized economy, are ready to work in low-skilled and low-wage jobs due to a market segmented into two categories, the first attracting native workers. International labour migration in the second sector is characterized by competition among states to send and/or receive workers but also by recruitment that tends to reproduce racialized and gendered stereotypes as well as discriminatory practices. For instance, women tend to do the three Cs – cooking, caring and cleaning (Anderson & Anderson, 2000) – and, if combined with ethnicity, domestic workers from Bangladesh and the Philippines are perceived in the MENA region to be racially inferior (Jureidini and Moukarbel, 2004).

At the same time, the 'paradox of the liberal state' has seen states pursuing free trade and openness to regulating migration (Hollifield, 2006) and signing up to several UN and international conventions that protect migrations and refugees. One example is the 1951 Geneva Convention on the Status of Refugees and its *principle of non-refoulement*. Article 33(1) of the Convention stipulates indeed that 'no Contracting State shall expel or return ("*refouler*") a refugee in any manner whatsoever to the frontiers of territories where his life or freedom would be threatened on account of his race, religion, nationality, membership of a particular social group or political opinion' (UNHCR, 1951).

Second, migration governance is torn between two contradictory logics. On the first hand, so-called 'remote control' policies have externalized the control of borders and people to third countries. The image of 'fortress Europe' illustrates the EU's restrictive policy towards irregular migration and economic migration, along with its requests that third countries take back irregular migrants through EU readmission agreements. But we have seen similar experiments of remote control in Australia and North America (Zaiotti, 2016). On the other hand, 'root causes' policies rely on development aid and the promotion of norms such as international protection (Wolff, 2017). The 'root causes of migration' logic follows a normative approach, promoting cooperation with third countries to tackle the 'push and pull factors' that incentivize migrants to leave their countries. Development aid strengthens capacity building but also fosters international norms on migration. Trade and foreign direct investment support the creation of jobs and support development through diasporas. This approach, also known as the 'migration–development nexus' (Nyberg Sorensen et al., 2002), is at the heart of the UN High-Level Dialogue on International Migration and regional consultative processes such as the Khartoum Process and the Rabat Process (also known as the Euro-African Dialogue on Migration and Development).

Migration policies are thus often designed from either a security or a development perspective, and mostly within a national setting. These obsolete conceptualizations, which apply to the way SSG/R has been designed and practised since the 1990s, ignore that migration is transnational and that people's mobility is a cross-sectoral challenge that mobilizes a whole array of public policies. Considering migration from a public policy perspective involves three main dimensions. First, it is about understanding policy processes and how best to integrate migration in the policy cycle of a country. The focus is then on actors, processes and instruments. In a way, this is a similar approach to what in the past 20 years has been done with the mainstreaming of environment or gender in public policies. Second, an evaluative approach is interested into how well different public policies perform their objectives in relation to migration. Evidence-based policymaking then is central to this dimension. Third, a normative dimension questions what the tasks are that public policies should perform in relation to migration.

These three dimensions are particularly relevant when rethinking the SSG/R–migration nexus. Instead of focusing merely on understanding why states, or the EU, want to externalize their controls (Zaiotti, 2016; Boswell, 2003) or how third countries may abuse their negotiating position (Reslow and Vink, 2015; Wolff, 2014), this paper explores how the security sector should address migration and how states should coordinate transnationally from an SSG/R perspective to have a protective effect on migrants. Although the focus is mostly on state structures when thinking about reforms leading towards a better SSG/R, this paper shows that local and transnational agency of different actors including migrants and refugees should be better integrated in SSG/R design and implementation. SSG/R can have a preventive and protective effect for vulnerable populations on the move since security sector actors (the judiciary, law enforcement, independent oversight bodies etc.) are part of the solution towards good migration governance that is safe and recognizes migrants and refugees as right-bearers that should be protected and enhanced by SSG actors.

CHAPTER 3

Conceptualizing Security Sector Governance (SSG) and Migration

3.1 What is SSG/R?

Various definitions of SSR prevail in the literature, and it is often understood and used in different ways by different users of the concept (Hänggi, 2009). Initially coined in the 1990s, it has been used at times to understand the modernization, transformation, reconstruction or development of the security sector. However, 'since the mid-2000's the concept has come to encompass security and justice sector reform' (DCAF, 2018). More specifically, the OECD Development Assistance Committee has agreed upon the following definition:

Box 3: Definition of security sector reform

Security sector reform means transforming the security sector/system, which includes all the actors, their roles, responsibilities and actions, so that they work together to manage and operate the system in a manner that is more consistent with democratic norms and sound principles of good governance, and thus contributes to a well-functioning security framework. (DCAF, 2018)

SSR usually leads to achieving the following goals:

1. Improv[ing] the democratic oversight of the security and justice system and its components.

How to cite this book chapter:
Wolff, S. 2021. *The Security Sector Governance–Migration Nexus: Rethinking how Security Sector Governance matters for migrants' rights.* Pp. 11–16. London: Ubiquity Press. DOI: https://doi .org/10.5334/bcl.c. License: CC-BY-NC

2. Improv[ing] the effective management of the security and justice system.
3. Strengthen[ing] the security and justice system's effectiveness in delivering services (DCAF, 2018).

It has been more broadly conceived as:

> the political and technical process of improving state and human security by making security provision, management and oversight more effective and more accountable, within a framework of democratic civilian control, rule of law and respect for human rights. The goal of SSR is to apply the principles of good governance to the security sector. (DCAF, 2015: 2)

SSR is seen to be 'functionally ambitious because it seeks to integrate activities such as defense, intelligence, police and judicial reform that in the past were conceived and administered as separate activities' (Bryden and Scherrer, 2012: 8). It is possible to distinguish between narrow and broader understandings of SSR. A narrow understanding:

> reflects state-centric understandings of security, focusing on those public sector institutions responsible for the provision of internal and external security, as well as on the civilian bodies relevant for their management, oversight and control. An expanded understanding … would include justice institutions … in recognition of the linkages and the complementary relationship between security and justice. (Hänggi, 2009)

An even broader approach also includes non-state actors such as private actors involved in the delivery.

Security sector governance (SSG) brings the additional dimension of not only considering the state actor and state-centric structures and institutions involved in the provision of security and justice but also involves principles of transparency and accountability. Accordingly, 'good SSG

Box 4: Principles of security sector governance

Accountability: there are clear expectations for security provision, and independent authorities oversee whether these expectations are met and impose sanctions if they are not met.

Transparency: information is freely available and accessible to those who will be affected by decisions and their implementation.

Rule of law: all persons and institutions, including the state, are subject to laws that are known publicly, enforced impartially and consistent with international and national human rights norms and standards.

Participation: all men and women of all backgrounds have the opportunity to participate in decision-making and service provision on a free, equitable and inclusive basis, either directly or through legitimate representative institutions.

Responsiveness: institutions are sensitive to the different security needs of all parts of the population and perform their missions in the spirit of a culture of service.

Effectiveness: institutions fulfil their respective roles, responsibilities and missions to a high professional standard.

Efficiency: institutions make the best possible use of public resources in fulfilling their respective roles, responsibilities and missions (DCAF, 2015: 3).

means applying the principles of good governance to a state's security sector. Good SSG is based on the idea that the security sector should be held to the same high standards of public service delivery as other public sector service providers' (DCAF, 2015: 3). Governance means that the delivery of the security sector happens with non-state actors and can be channelled through formal and informal ways.

However, a quick review of the literature shows that SSG/R is a narrowly conceived concept that has more trouble coping with transnational issues such as migration owing to the inherent nature of its actors, which are mostly representatives of governments and states. They are also mostly in charge of national security, sometimes beyond, owing to developments like Schengen in the EU, but have little expertise in transnational operations and cooperation. SSR is also predominantly an external donor concept implemented by external actors in post-conflict reconstruction and peace-/state-building efforts (Wingens, 2016: 106). One of the key points of contention is whether SSG/R should be implemented by external actors and/or domestic actors. There is indeed a predominant 'donor-driven reform narrative' that ignores the local context and needs and is embedded within a very Western liberal understanding of the nation state (Ibid, 107). This is necessarily less adapted to transnational issues like migration, which has seen the involvement of SSG/R actors through an excessive militarization of the issue.

One of the main challenges in revamping the SSG/R–migration nexus is that, while SSG is mostly designed at the national level through reforms that require national plans and ownership, migration remains inherently a transnational phenomenon. Border crossings challenge nation states and are mostly intra-regional. Many of the current governance challenges are the result of the externalization of migration policies by destination countries to origin and transit countries. These policies have devoted little attention to anchoring migration policies within democratic accountability and how these policies should also include training and assistance of foreign security forces in managing migration and following the principles of SSG.

Before moving to the reasons why SSG/R should revise its relationship with migration, it is important to stress that, at the international level, the reflection remains rather scattered. In particular, the 2018 Global Compact on Migration never properly speaks about the importance of SSG/R but mentions different aspects of it that are key to migration governance.

Box 5: SSG/R–migration and the Global Compact: relevant guiding principles (United Nations, 2018)

'*Rule of law and due process.* The Global Compact recognizes that respect for the rule of law, due process and access to justice are fundamental to all aspects of migration governance. This means that the State, public and private institutions and entities, as well as persons themselves, are accountable to laws that are publicly promulgated, equally enforced and independently adjudicated, and are consistent with international law;

Human rights. The Global Compact is based on international human rights law and upholds the principles of non-regression and non-discrimination. By implementing the Global Compact, we ensure effective respect for and protection and fulfilment of the human rights of all migrants, regardless of their migration status, across all stages of the migration cycle. We also reaffirm the commitment to eliminate all forms of discrimination, including racism, xenophobia and intolerance, against migrants and their families;

Gender-responsive. The Global Compact ensures that the human rights of women, men, girls and boys are respected at all stages of migration, that their specific needs are properly understood and addressed and that they are empowered as agents of change. It mainstreams a gender perspective and promotes gender equality and the empowerment of all women and girls, recognizing their independence, agency and leadership in order to move away from addressing migrant women primarily through a lens of victimhood;

Child-sensitive. The Global Compact promotes existing international legal obligations in relation to the rights of the child, and upholds the principle of the best interests of the child at all times, as a primary consideration in all situations concerning children in the context of international migration, including unaccompanied and separated children;

Whole-of-government approach. The Global Compact considers that migration is a multidimensional reality that cannot be addressed by one government policy sector alone. To develop and implement effective migration policies and practices, a whole-of-government approach is needed to ensure horizontal and vertical policy coherence across all sectors and levels of government;

Whole-of-society approach. The Global Compact promotes broad multi-stakeholder partnerships to address migration in all its dimensions by including migrants, diasporas, local communities, civil society, academia, the private sector, parliamentarians, trade unions, national human rights institutions, the media and other relevant stakeholders in migration governance'.

Among the objectives listed for safe, orderly and regular migration, the following are directly relevant for SSG/R.

Box 6: The Global Compact on Migration and SSG/R-relevant objectives (United Nations, 2018)

12 out of 23 objectives are directly relevant for SSG/R
4. Ensure that all migrants have proof of legal identity and adequate documentation.
7. Address and reduce vulnerabilities in migration.
8. Save lives and establish coordinated international efforts on missing migrants.
9. Strengthen the transnational response to smuggling of migrants.
10. Prevent, combat and eradicate trafficking in persons in the context of international migration.
11. Manage borders in an integrated, secure and coordinated manner.
12. Strengthen certainty and predictability in migration procedures for appropriate screening, assessment and referral.
13. Use migration detention only as a measure of last resort and work towards alternatives.
15. Provide access to basic services for migrants.
17. Eliminate all forms of discrimination and promote evidence-based public discourse to shape perceptions of migration.
21. Cooperate in facilitating safe and dignified return and readmission, as well as sustainable reintegration.
23. Strengthen international cooperation and global partnerships for safe, orderly and regular migration.

3.2 The relevance of the migration–SSG/R nexus

The literature on the migration–SSG/R nexus is scarce, mostly confined to either the externalization of destination countries' migration and border policies to transit and origin countries or the narrow consideration of police and border forces' role in controlling migration. It is nonetheless obvious that migration and SSG/R are intimately linked and require a renewed conceptualization. Migrants and refugees and the security sector are constantly interacting, and it is surprising that no further unpacking of that relationship has been conducted in order to improve migration governance.

This global trend of externalization of migration and border controls raises ethical and moral challenges, even where security forces decide to 'export' surveillance technologies. In general, there has been a disconnection of migration policies, treated as a security threat, from apprehending migration cooperation as a way to improve good SSG. A decentred approach to migration governance also involves revisiting the role of ethics and morals, including of SSG/R at the border.

This is key as weak SSG in origin countries can lead to instability and a lack of trust in police and the judicial sector and thus contribute to the reasons that lead an individual to leave their country. In transit countries, the absence of judicial guarantees and respect for the rule of law make migrants' and refugees' transit throughout the country dangerous and full of uncertainties. In destination countries, strong SSG plays a crucial role in the respect for migrants' and refugees' rights but also in their safety and societal integration. This involves improving local ownership, to engage with local communities in order to advance accountability, 'public trust and confidence' (Gordon, 2014: 1). Migration here poses another set of challenges in addition to engaging with traditional local and national communities. In general, migrants are considered foreign, aliens to the national community, to which they need to prove their rights and show that they deserve equal treatment. The fact that irregular migration is being criminalized in many parts of the world means that SSG is also interacting with migrants in order to stop them and detain them as if they were criminals. Local communities and diasporas might be suspected and convicted of helping irregular migration, and the security sector may very often approach these migrants as problematic. The role of SSG is thus key, especially in destination countries, to protect migrants and refugees against widespread xenophobia sentiments.

Human trafficking is particularly relevant to the discussion on SSG as it is a 'human rights issue, a violation of labour and migration laws, and as undermining national and international security through its links to organised crime and corruption' (Bastick and Grimm, 2007: 7). The governance of human trafficking has changed considerably over the past 20 years, and in particular since the signing of the UN Protocol to Prevent, Suppress and Punish Trafficking in Persons (TIP) in 2000, which was the first meaningful instrument on the topic. Various instruments have proliferated since then and 'recent years have witnessed the emergence and spread of novel forms of soft or voluntary rule making developed by intergovernmental organizations (IGOs) and private actors' (Gómez-Mera, 2017: 303). Initiatives in human trafficking have, however, not necessarily been successful, in part due to the fact that:

> the implementation of TIP rules and norms remains uneven and driven by states' security and domestic political priorities. At the same time, recent times have witnessed an increase in TIP in conflict zones, where traffickers take advantage of economic desperation and institutional weakness. In these contexts, both interstate laws and transnational private and hybrid regulations against TIP and forced labour prove largely ineffective. (Gómez-Mera, 2017: 322)

The security sector is thus importantly involved in the fight against human trafficking and the fight against corruption is necessarily a crucial step towards making sure security sector actors are not involved in human trafficking and that criminal justice adequately addresses this issue. The challenge is also to make a clear difference between trafficking, smugglers and humanitarian workers, who in situations of rescue at sea in the Mediterranean can be sanctioned on the basis of article 1(2) of Council Directive 2002/90/EC, which defines the facilitation of unauthorized entry, transit and residence and allows Member States to criminalize citizens engaged in providing humanitarian assistance to migrants in irregular situations, including aid workers performing search and rescue activities at sea. Good practices such as the development of a search and rescue code of conduct by NGOs is the type of initiative to be followed.[3]

In addition, it is impossible to pursue a self-reflective process on SSG/R and migration without considering the ethical and moral challenges inherently linked to this reconceptualization. Indeed, over the past few years, international migration governance has somehow become a technical and technocratic object where 'policy instruments' govern migration policies and are implemented by various security agencies such as the UK Border Agency and the European Border and Coast Guard Agency and has seen the predominant role of home affairs and/or interior ministries, as well as the police. Yet, in recent years, and in particular since the 2015 'crisis', debates about the moral duties to save migrants, to rescue them at sea, mobilizing emotions and ethical arguments have arisen and are used in various ways by different security sector actors. These arguments also vary across countries and serve different political purposes. One key element that has arisen is how border guards see themselves as professionals conducting rescues and protecting lives vs. what they sometimes see as 'amateurism' on the part of NGOs, leading to a 'competition among military forces and non-state humanitarians regarding rescue operations' (Karadag, 2020: 15). This sometimes contributes to create moral hierarchies and seeing some SSG actors as morally superior to others, because they are 'better professionals'. On the contrary, a real decentred rethinking of SSG/R should be about how to work together for the benefit of migrants. Similarly, if one considers a decentred perspective on migration and SSG/R, this necessarily means moving away from Eurocentric understandings of migration and seeing that migration is inherently a transnational phenomenon that affects all countries in the world. It also means that more illiberal states are managing migration and, for instance, in the case of Turkish coast guards, 'operating on the Aegean Sea without any witness of a non-state actor' (Karadag, 2020: 16), leading to more potential for manipulation by border guards.

---

[3] Code of conduct available at https://www.humanrightsatsea.org/2017/03/31/european-parliament-human-rights-at-sea-outlines-voluntary-sar-ngo-code-of-conduct/.

CHAPTER 4

The SSG/R–Migration Nexus and Migrants' Journeys

This chapter reviews how SSG/R plays out in people's journeys between their countries of emigration/immigration and countries of departure/destination. I debate first the now oft-used typology of origin, transit and destination countries (4.1). I then review what the link is between SSG/R in countries of origin (4.2), transit (4.3) and destination (4.4). I end by reviewing the role that SSG/R plays in sites of exceptions such as refugee camps and detention facilities, which can be found in all countries (4.5).

4.1 Origin, transit and destination countries: typological challenges

A decentred move to better understanding how SSG/R can be conceptualized to benefit migrants is probably to question the now very widely used classification of origin, transit and destination countries. Because this classification over-simplifies trends, prioritizing the needs and views of destination countries, often thought to be in the Global North, I prefer to use the terms emigration, immigration and departure/destination. Boucher and Gest suggest that we can improve typologies of migration regimes by considering the 'broadly democratic nature of an immigration regime', for instance by 'using both Freedom House and Polity IV instruments' (Boucher and Gest, 2014).

This typology ignores complex movements around the world. Let's consider the example of the Gulf countries. They are a destination for migrants from the Horn of Africa but also from Asia to come and work in the construction sector and as domestic helpers, with a strong issue

How to cite this book chapter:
Wolff, S. 2021. *The Security Sector Governance–Migration Nexus: Rethinking how Security Sector Governance matters for migrants' rights*. Pp. 17–25. London: Ubiquity Press. DOI: https://doi
.org/10.5334/bcl.d. License: CC-BY-NC

of forced labour and exploitation. Gulf countries have not known huge emigration, with only some limited movements of skilled migrants abroad to Europe, Australia or India. In fact, the United Arab Emirates (UAE) instead face a problem of population imbalance, with more non-national residents than the national population born in the country (Mansour, 2015: 308). This situation also applies to countries such as Singapore, which has aimed at attracting high-skilled migrants, leading to a rise from 991,500 migrants in 1995 to more than 2.7 million in 2017 (IOM, 2018).

It is therefore quite a complex task to categorize countries in such definite categories as origin, transit or destination countries as the immigration situation has changed historically and very much depends on labour needs and push and pull factors, as well as public migration policies from governments. Other countries such as Japan, for instance, are confronted with a demographic gap and, in spite of the clear need for foreign workers to maintain the expansive Japanese welfare policy started in the 1990s,

> policy reforms have been slow and are far from achieving their goals. Most Japanese citizens are highly ambivalent about opening up the country to immigration, and the idea of immigration and multicultural societies remains disconnected from that of a shared national identity premised on ethnic and cultural homogeneity. (Peng, 2016: 278)

In the field of migration policies, scholars and statisticians have long wrestled with a lack of comparative data. The main reason is that for a very long time, given that the focus has been on traditional destination countries in the 'North', most of the gathered data, and the institutions supported to gather this data, has remained located in OECD countries. There is in general a lack of understanding but also of data on migration policies in the Global South, which is, however, hosting 86% of refugees and 48% of current immigrant stock (Boucher and Gest, 2014: 3). For a very long time there has been also an association between destination countries and democratic states. Yet, many of the new immigration-receiving countries are non-democratic, which raises the need to reframe typologies away from being democratic-state-centric because naturalization/citizenship is out of the question.

4.2 Countries of emigration

Although there are many reasons for people to leave their countries of origin that we are not going to review in depth here, the absence of strong SSG, which involves accountability, transparency, the rule of law, participation, responsiveness, effectiveness and efficiency, is one of the reasons leading to instability, poor economic prospects and the motivation for migrants and refugees to leave the country. Research has shown that there is a direct correlation between weak state structures and IDPs since, in the absence of security, 'displaced individuals will not voluntarily return in great numbers [in their home areas]' (England, 2012: 4). Indeed, it is important to stress that, if state structures are unable to provide security to citizens, or constitute a source of instability, leading to violence, this is one of the factors driving people to leave their country or to be internally displaced.

If we are speaking of war-torn countries with poor SSG, the level of justice-sensitive SSG is relatively low. Unsurprisingly, the main nationalities of first-time asylum applicants in the EU 28 in 2018 and 2019 were Syrian, Afghan and Venezuelan. All these countries score rather poorly on democracy, rule of law and adequate SSG (Figure 2).

Similarly, in the US, first-time applicants for asylum between 2015 and 2017 were mostly from Venezuela. But in Table 1 we see countries like China and Mexico, which are not (post-)conflict countries but where we can suspect that authoritarianism (for China) and violent crime (for Mexico) motivate people to flee the country.

Countries of origin of (non-EU) asylum seekers in the EU-27 Member States, 2018 and 2019
(thousands of first-time applicants)

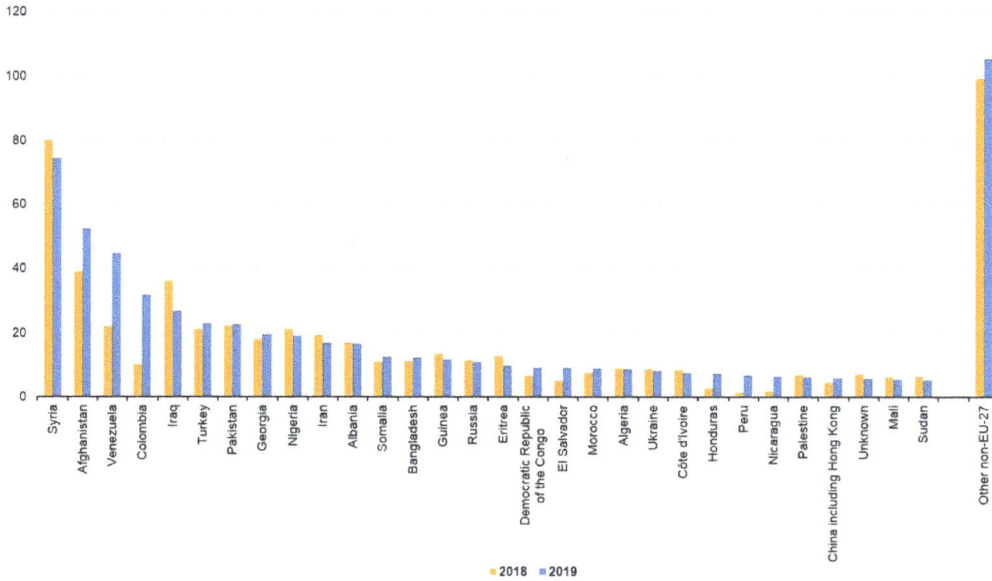

Source: Eurostat (online data code: migr_asyappctza)

eurostat

Figure 2: Statistics on asylum seekers in the European Union.

Country	2017		2016		2015	
	Number	**Percent**	**Number**	**Percent**	**Number**	**Percent**
Total	139,801	100.0	115,433	100.0	83,032	100.0
Venezuela	27,579	19.7	14,792	12.8	5,664	6.8
China, People's Republic	16,792	12.0	16,508	14.3	13,877	16.7
Guatemala	12,175	8.7	10,720	9.3	8,277	10.0
Mexico	11,941	8.5	14,660	12.7	8,820	10.6
El Salvador	11,913	8.5	9,444	8.2	7,133	8.6
Honduras	6,978	5.0	5,698	4.9	5,147	6.2
India	4,057	2.9	3,230	2.8	2,276	2.7
Haiti	3,860	2.8	3,004	2.6	1,918	2.3
Colombia	2,250	1.9	1,395	1.2	820	1.0
Russia	2,649	1.9	1,909	1.7	1,447	1.7
All other countries, incl. unknown	39,207	28.0	34,073	29.5	27,653	33.3

Table 1: Affirmative asylum cases filed with USCIS by country of nationality: FY 2015 to 2017.
Source: US Department of Homeland Security (2019).

Countries of origin therefore involve a wide spectrum of situation when it comes to SSG/R. Often violence seems to be a common denominator to these countries (including in Russia, which still is one of the main countries of origin for asylum application in the EU and in the US). Interestingly enough, violence is not necessarily always directed towards the lower strata of the population in countries of origin. In Colombia, researchers have shown that:

> emigration is more likely to be initiated by those with higher education, those with network connections to migrants, and during periods of greater violence and increased police presence. Although violence acts powerfully to determine when people migrate, the geographic distribution of social capital determines where they go. (Silva and Massey, 2014: 162)

In other words, people migrate where they have networks and diasporas.

In countries of destination, there is a tendency, which was particularly highlighted during the 2015 crisis in Europe, to portray refugees 'as violent actors, when strong anecdotal evidence suggests that they are generally the victims of abuse' (Gineste and Savun, 2019: 134). A recent database on refugee-related violence in their host state, named POSVAR (the Political and Societal Violence by and against Refugees), has developed a 'cross-national, time-series data on refugees' involvement in acts of physical violence in their host state, either as the victims or the perpetrators of violence, individually or collectively, in all countries between 1996 and 2015' (Ibid: 134). This database is helpful to reverse the perspective and to identify whether there is a link between SSG actors in countries of origin and refugee-related violence (Ibid: 135).

In addition, in countries of origin, and probably more in post-conflict countries, SSG/R also suffers from a lack of professionals and expertise. Indeed, the security sector, sometimes

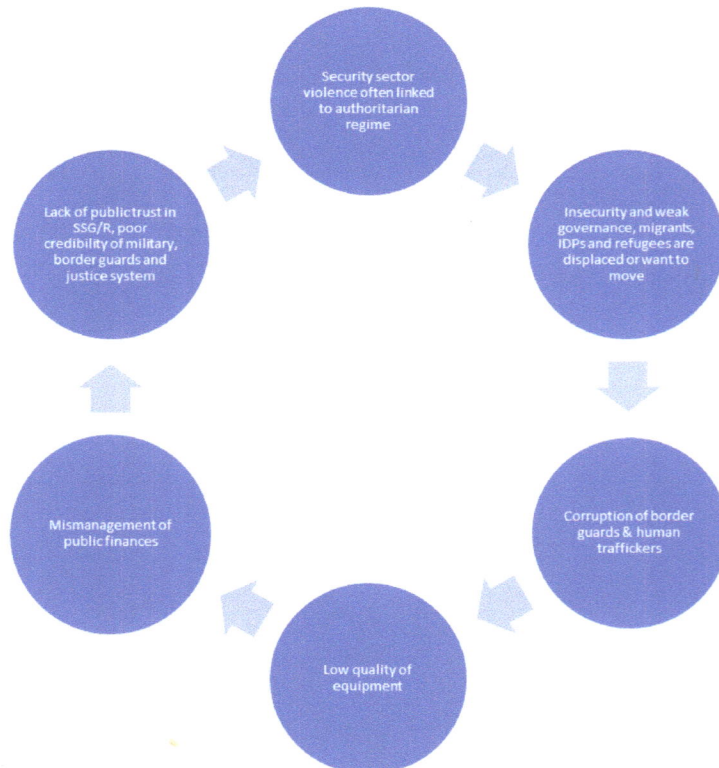

Figure 3: The non-virtuous cycle of the SSG/R–migration nexus.

demobilized and sometimes counting themselves as IDPs, has led 'to a knowledge and capacity gap in security institutions' (England, 2012: 4). And therefore, as in the case of IDPs, a country with highly educated people who leave to migrate or escape difficult situations also leads to a brain-drain and a gap in the skills and expertise to reform local security institutions.

Figure 3 shows that there is a vicious circle in countries of origin between week SSG/R and migration. The presence of bad SSG/R can be a motivation in creating movements of IDPs, especially if there is a conflict, but also in inciting people to leave the country owing to the insecurity and weak governance in the country.

4.3 Fragmented journeys: the problem with 'transit migrants' and 'transit countries'

A country of transit is one in which 'migration flows (regular or irregular) move' (IOM, 2011). Against conventional assumptions, countries of transit are not only located in developing countries; many countries have become 'transit countries', including in Europe.

More broadly, it is important to caution against the use of 'transit migration', which is not a clear-cut category and is also a 'blurred and politicised concept' (Düvell, 2012: 415). This categorization is worrisome as many countries will then consider that individuals are just crossing their countries on the way to another destination and, therefore, will not take any responsibility to deal with migrants[4] and refugees and to provide the necessary resources for protecting their rights. It gives this idea of temporariness, that migrants and refugees are not there for long, and thus can lead to dismissive public policies. From the point of view of destination countries such as EU Member States, transit countries are mostly targeted in terms of externalization policies that aim at preventing unwanted migration. The term 'transit' is used by the EU to cooperate with neighbouring countries and ask them to take their own responsibilities in sending migrants back home. Yet there is little acknowledgement among policymakers in destination countries that the creation of the category of 'transit countries' is a direct consequence of surveillance and border control policies that push migrants and refugees to 'turn to dangerous routes or who are trapped or stranded in third countries [as] a direct consequence of EU immigration restrictions' (Düvell, 2012: 415).

Box 7: The problem with 'transit migration'

The emergence of the concept is closely related to political motivations; indeed the concept is often negatively connoted and highly politicised. In discourse analysis it would probably be considered a threat frame similar to that of 'illegal migration'. The way it is applied by some supranational, international and intergovernmental organisations is often grossly simplified and misleading (Düvell, 2012: 415).

Although the term may look innovative, it does not challenge but actually reinforces the notion that migratory moves have fixed starting and end points, and, by doing so, it essentializes the transit space by reducing it to a 'through' space (Collyer and Haas, 2012: 479).

Indeed, if Hungary or Turkey considers itself permanently a 'country of transit', then one may wonder how meaningful reforms, including improving the SSG–migration nexus, can realistically take place. Countries that continue to identify themselves as such thus avoid their responsibilities

---

[4] The term 'migrant' is generically applied as it can cover irregular migrants but also situations where migrants have entered legally to work seasonally or temporarily but then may overstay their visas.

to provide the 'opportunity structures *en route*' that are essential for migrants and will affect importantly their journeys (Brekke and Brochmann, 2015: 145). These structures include reception centres, adequate temporary housing arrangements, healthcare etc. The absence of adequate policies also leads human traffickers to easily abuse the situation.

Various studies have highlighted the increased risks of bribery and corruption. This happens from the start of the journey, with traffickers, but also 'to exit refugee camps, guards and security personnel are often bribed' (OECD, 2015: 3). One of the core business of corruption consists in fraud around travel documents, which might involve 'bribing the relevant public administration in charge' (Ibid) but also buying 'passports and visas through corrupt officials in embassies' (Ibid). Yet again, seeing corruption as mostly a transit country issue is misleading. Corruption happens on all borders, but in countries of origin or destination, owing to weaker legislation and lower working conditions and salaries of border guards, the risks are possibly higher. It is also important to highlight that 'corruption at borders manifests itself through various forms, including petty bribery, bureaucratic corruption, misappropriation, organised crime related corruption and political corruption' (Chêne, 2018: 1). In destination countries such as those in Europe, corruption has been denounced in relation to 'golden visa' initiatives, where countries offer citizenship or residents to people who want to invest in their countries. In Europe this concerns '13 countries: Austria, Belgium, Bulgaria, Cyprus, Greece, Latvia, Lithuania, Malta, Monaco, Portugal, Spain, Switzerland, and the United Kingdom. Hungary ran a controversial Golden Visa programme from 2013 to 2017' (Transparency International, 2019). A report by Transparency International has revealed that these forms of investment attract the wrong type of money and 'represent a potential threat to the fight against cross-border corruption. Without sufficient integrity checks in place, they constitute an easy back door for the corrupt' (Ibid, 2019).

Libya is a country that typically fits this category of 'transit country' and where probably the situation of ongoing civil conflict, the presence of militias, a weak legislative framework and low conditions for border guards makes it an explosive combination. In fact, the security sector is itself involved in smuggling and human trafficking: 'accounts of migrants who have transited through Libya testify to the general tolerance of the transportation of migrants into and from Libya, along with active participation and profiteering by Libyan security agencies' (Baldwin-Edwards and Lutterbeck, 2018: 4). The Horn of Africa is also of particular concern here. Although the number of Eritreans, for instance, has dropped sharply, with 7,272 crossings by sea in 2017, due in part to the situation in Libya, they represented 15% of sea crossings to reach Europe in 2014.[5] This is notwithstanding the number of Eritrean refugees in Ethiopia and Sudan bringing the diaspora to about half a million, and making the country of six million people "one of the world's fastest-emptying nations" according to the *Wall Street Journal* (Laub, 2016). Overall, among the main nationalities attempting to cross towards Europe, the top 10 nationalities that enter clandestinely at EU border crossing points matches a list of countries where state failure is a top concern. Yet, categorizing Libya as a transit country can be pretty unhelpful given the wide fragmentation of personal situations and also the fact that it can devoid the Libyan authorities from addressing their core responsibilities in terms of migrants' and refugees' rights.

I therefore agree with Collyer and Haas that in order to raise awareness among SSR actors a more dynamic understanding of migration and typologies of countries could probably be useful. Collyer has, for instance, introduced the concept of 'fragmented journeys' to better understand the reality of migrants wrongly labelled in transit:

---

[5] According to Frontex (2017). Risk Analysis for 2018 out of a total of sea borders crossings of 220188, 34 323 were coming out of Eritreans. Accessed on 4 October 2018 at https://frontex.europa.eu/assets/Publications/Risk _Analysis/Risk_Analysis/Risk_Analysis_for_2018.pdf.

This linearity imposes fixed points of origin and destination on much more complex and dynamic lived realities so that everything in between, perhaps many years of wandering, becomes 'transit'. For those people involved in this process, as we have demonstrated, 'transit' is a totally inadequate term. Yet 'transience' or 'wandering' suggests a lack of purpose that is not accurate either. (Collyer and Haas, 2012: 478)

Migrants are not 'lost in transit' or 'lost in translation' with no purpose. This would be overlooking the role of migration policies and also their own agency in determining the journey they are undertaking. This fragmented perspective could also lead to stop labelling countries as 'transit countries' and thus the risk of watering down efforts to raise awareness among state authorities and policymakers of the relevance of migration and refugees.

4.4 Countries of destination or host societies

Although the term 'countries of destination' is often used, I suggest using the term 'host societies' as being probably more accurate and following a decentred perspective that is both less Western-oriented and less state-centric. Countries of destination are often thought to be the countries where a better life is possible, in advanced democracies and with liberal practices towards migrants and refugees. But countries of destination also happen to be in the Global South since there are also important intra-regional migration flows. According to the UN, 'Nowadays in South America, the number of intra-regional immigrants is converging with the number of South American emigrants residing elsewhere in the world' (Cerruti, 2020). These growing intra-regional movements are also accompanied by a more diverse socio-economic profile of migrants. For instance, Argentina and Bolivia are no longer the only main countries of destination. Thus, '[i]n Chile, immigration almost tripled in a decade. In Ecuador immigration grew considerably mainly due to its dollarized economy and the violence experienced in Colombia; and in Uruguay, a traditionally emigration country, immigration almost double[d] as well' (Cerruti, 2020). In the Economic Community of West African States (ECOWAS), 84% of migration flows take place within that same region (Lanneau, 2015: 5) and we see that all ECOWAS member states are countries of origin and destination.

In host societies, a good SSG is a prerequisite to ensure safe journeys, the respect for migrants' and refugees' fundamental rights, including that they are being given the right to apply for asylum and that, when they are in a period of detention waiting for their papers, they are being provided with safe and dignified conditions.

In host societies, like in countries of emigration/departure, one of the key issues is violence against refugees, which is on the rise, requiring the mobilization of SSG at all levels. Anti-refugee movements have been quite vocal and gained increased visibility. Gineste and Savun's study shows that violence against refugees in host societies is always higher than violence by refugees. But this has become particularly striking since 2010.

This study is particularly relevant as it confirms that the 'states and their agents are the primary perpetrators of violence against refugees' (Gineste and Savun, 2019: 7). They illustrate their argument by mentioning the '2004 massacre of at least 166 Congolese refugees by the Forces for National Liberation (FNL) or the killing of 107 Tutsi refugees from the Democratic Republic of the Congo (DRC) by Rwanda Hutu militiamen in 1997' (Gineste and Savun, 2019: 7).

More recent examples of such violence happen when host societies do not allow refugees and migrants to enter the country. This occurred, for instance, during the 'caravan' of migrants on the US–Mexican border, with border guards firing tear gas, including at children. Similarly, border guards and their agencies have also been blamed for the death of migrants in detention, such as after the death of eight-year-old Felipe Gomez Alonzo, who was in custody under US Customs and Border Protection (Eaton, 2018).

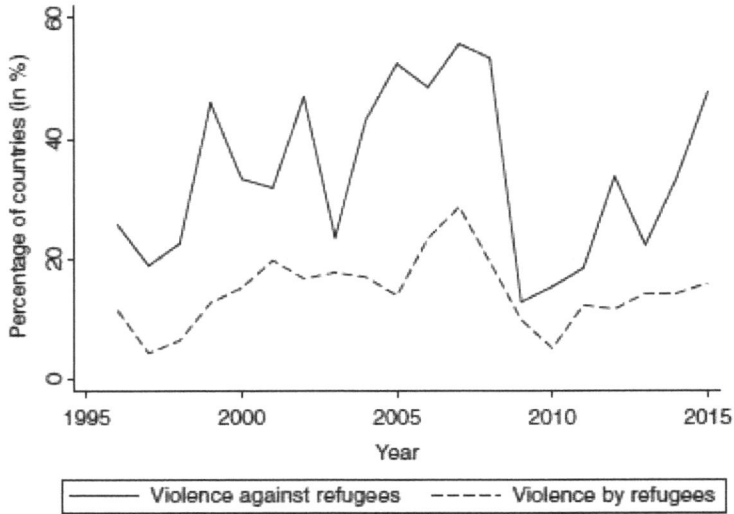

Figure 4: Violence against refugees.

Incidences of police violence and abuse of authority have also been widely reported, including in liberal democracies. The Dublin Convention and the policy issues surrounding the non-realistic implementation of the principle of the country of first entry have meant that some security sector actors in Southern Europe have been the most exposed to migrants and refugees. In Italy, the Italian police and port authorities have resorted to coercing refugees to provide their fingerprints and be photographed and registered (Davies, Isakjee and Dhesi, 2017: 1272). Research has concluded that 'a majority of refugees interviewed for this research felt they had been "abandoned" by European state authorities' (Ibid: 1272). This may undermine the trust in state structures.

While some might be seen as wanted migrants, because they bring skills, issues of integration continue to be a big issue. This is the case in many parts of the world. Within the ECOWAS region, the 'vast majority of foreigners work in low-skilled positions in the informal sector' (Devillard et al., 2015: 29), which thus presents little opportunities for regularization. Also, migrants from ECOWAS countries tend to have a low level of education (Devillard et al., 2015: 34). This is why, in spite of the 1979 ECOWAS Protocol relating to the Free Movement of Persons, the right of residence and establishment, which allows for a right of entry and the abolition of visa requirements for a 90-day stay period, there has been slow 'progress … as regarding the Right of Residence, the Right of Establishment and access to employment' (Devillard et al., 2015: 3).

4.5 Refugee camps and detention facilities

Throughout their journeys, refugees, notably fleeing poverty, conflict or environmental hazards, will probably end up in a refugee camp. In destination countries, or countries at the periphery, they will have to wait for their asylum applications to be processed in 'hotspots' in the case of the EU such as the infamous Moria camp in Greece, destroyed by a fire in September 2020 on the island of Lesbos. Analysing the role of SSG in these spaces is particularly relevant as critical scholars see these camps and detention facilities as part of governmentality techniques that influence the imagined geopolitics of borders. Such literature emphasises how 'border work is performed at many locations' through outsourcing, offshoring, extra-territorialization and externalization (Mamadouh, 2015: 58). Camps are buffer zones, also seen in the case of the EU as 'limboscapes' (Ferrer-Gallardo and Albet-Mas, 2016). These camps are also important sites of social formation and as such have been instrumental in the quest for their demands, such as in the case of the Sahrawi in the Polisario Front camps (Fiddian-Qasmiyeh, 2014). They can also be spaces where practices of spatial disobedience happen whereby 'asylum-seekers refuse to comply with the restrictive conditions established by [EU] asylum and migration policies, enacting and claiming freedom of choice' (Tazzioli, 2017: 3), for instance by refusing to have their fingerprints taken. Refugees are also active political subjects as they organize themselves in the camps and show resilience. Drawing from the work of Agamben, Ilcan and Rygiel show that neo-liberalism has, through the empowerment of the refugees and IDPs living there, transformed these camps, which were supposed to be exceptional and temporary, not permanent, places where resiliency humanitarianism transforms them into 'residents'. They highlight the risks of 'depoliticization' and 'complacency' to turn refugee camps into permanent structures where refugees are 'encouraged to accept rather than resist, their ominous living conditions in camps' (Ilcan and Rygiel, 2015: 348). Understanding the role of SSG actors within these trends is also key when it comes to managing camps and possible protests in refugee camps.

CHAPTER 5

Mapping the Field: The Role of SSG Actors and Institutions in Migration

SSG actors and institutions are in constant interaction with migrants and refugees. Let's consider how different security sector actors interact with migrants and refugees.

5.1 The military

In the country of departure, the military can be involved in a conflict that leads to instability and forces people to leave the country. Military and paramilitary conflicts and wars lead to forced migration. For instance, after the intervention in Libya, the thinking about the consequences of taking down the Qadhafi regime with the rise of tribal and rival militias has led to forced migration and internally displaced people. Both the dismantlement of the Qadhafi regime and the Syrian conflict certainly explain the post-Arab Spring influx of migrants and refugees ready to cross the Mediterranean Sea. Major regional geopolitical changes have led populations to flee conflict. Migratory patterns are also evolving rapidly due to the rise of socio-economic inequalities, poverty and climate change. Better planning and foresight when it comes to migration would be useful from a military perspective. But the problem is that it is not always clear in the mind of the military how they should integrate migration and when it should be conceived as a threat. '[W]hat represents the actual threat: is it a migrant, the number of migrants, the potential or perceived consequences of migration, the lack of capacity to respond to a migration crisis, or all of the above? The threat perception put forward in official documents lacks coherence' (Himmerich, 2018: 5).

The military is usually involved in two ways with migration: through the militarization of border control and through the development of humanitarian functions.

How to cite this book chapter:
Wolff, S. 2021. *The Security Sector Governance–Migration Nexus: Rethinking how Security Sector Governance matters for migrants' rights*. Pp. 27–49. London: Ubiquity Press. DOI: https://doi .org/10.5334/bcl.e. License: CC-BY-NC

First, during the migration 'crisis' of 2015–16 the military was mobilized in relation to migration in new ways following people's journeys through the Western Balkans. It led to new deployment and defence cooperation in Central Europe (Nemeth, 2018) on internal borders. Thus,

> almost 7 000 troops with significant amount of equipment and numerous vehicles were sent by Austria (1 600 troops), Bulgaria (140 troops), Hungary (4 500 troops) and Slovenia (700 troops) to their respective borders in order to help managing the migration crisis in 2015–2016. Since then their troops have been participating in patrolling the affected borders, supporting civilian authorities and building border fences (500 km by Hungary; 200 km by Slovenia; 150 km by Bulgaria, 4 km by Austria). Not surprisingly border control has become one of the core tasks of the armed forces of these countries. (Nemeth, 2018)

The new route had high-level implications too, as:

> the Central European Defense Cooperation (CEDC), which was created by Austria, Croatia, the Czech Republic, Hungary, Slovakia and Slovenia in 2010 to support smaller NATO and EU capability development projects through military cooperation, became the most relevant Central European platform for defense collaboration against irregular migration. (Nemeth, 2018)

Accordingly, 'during these meetings, the CEDC defense ministers agreed on enhanced intelligence sharing on irregular migration flows, providing material assistance to each other, developing shared situational awareness and effective coordination mechanisms' (Nemeth, 2018).

Then, the military has been importantly involved with humanitarian work. During the various stages of migrants' and refugees' journeys, the military is likely to be involved in the management of refugee camps, and have a duty to provide security to refugees. As outlined by a representative from the Lawyers Committee for Human Rights, this should involve:

> the minimum of coercion, and thus the minimum restriction of refugee human rights, should always be the first to be considered. Military rules of assessment and engagement, in addition to training and accountability structures, tend to harbor different implications for the human rights of refugees. Secondly, it is important to bear in mind that the mere presence of, or engagement with the military will directly diminish the civilian nature of a refugee settlement – a crucial principle of refugee protection. It is clear also that depending on whether national or multilateral military forces are involved, very different mandates and styles of action will have been taken into consideration. (Lawyers Committee for Human Rights, unknown: 4)

In countries of departure and of 'transit', the military can play a more specific role in refugee camps in two ways: '(a) bringing war criminals to justice and (b) separating combatants from refugees. The ability of the military to contribute to the process of bringing war criminals to justice under international humanitarian law has been broadly welcomed even by humanitarian NGOs' (Lawyers Committee for Human Rights, unknown: 4). The second element is really key as the mixing of combatants into refugee camps and maybe even later on into migratory flows may lead to a situation of insecurity for refugees in the camps, but also to situations of impunity. As explained above, this can only happen under very specific conditions and should take place under the central command of police or prosecutors with relevant experience and legal mandate.

The 'militarization' of refugee camps is a core challenge, including preserving their civilian nature. In this context,

> militarization refers to non-civilian attributes of refugee populated areas, including inflows of weapons, military training and recruitment. It also includes actions of refugees and/or

exiles who engage in non-civilian activity outside the refugee camp, yet who depend on assistance from refugees or international organizations. (Yu, 2002: 1)

International organizations such as the UNHCR and peacekeeping operations involving militaries from other countries might thus have to proceed to this separation to avoid the mixing of militias and armed elements into refugee camps. Thus, Yu reports that:

In October and November 2001 a group of Central African Republic soldiers (FACA) and their family members, totaling 1,220 people, were separated from a larger group of 25,000 refugees who had fled the Central African Republic (CAR). To prevent infiltration of armed elements into the refugee population, the ex-FACA and their dependents were relocated to a second site prior to encampment. This separation took place in the town of Congo in northwestern Democratic Republic of the Congo (DRC) and was led by the UNHCR with the support of the UN peacekeeping mission in the DRC (MONUC). (Yu: 2002: 1)

Box 8: Functions of the military in relation to migration

– patrolling borders.
– rescuing migrants at sea and involved in humanitarian emergencies through civil–ilitary coordination.
– protecting migrants in refugee camps.

5.2 Police forces

Next to have the monopoly of force, the police are law enforcement bodies that have the duty to protect property, the safety and the human rights of citizens and residents, including migrants and refugees, to ensure state security, and to maintain public order. There are different types of policing across the world and with different professional cultures, ranging from paramilitary forces (i.e. the *gendarmerie* in France or the Guardia Civil in Spain) to decentralized, community-oriented civilian police agencies. One of the main issues in relation to migrants and asylum seekers, depending on the status of the person and the country, is that police forces might be seen as a threat instead of as a trusted partner that protects migrants' and asylum seekers' rights.

Box 9: Functions of the police in relation to migration

– controlling people's immigration status.
– doing community policing in neighbourhoods with important immigrant communities.
– investigation of cases of human trafficking and human smuggling.
– enforcement of immigration laws.
– maintaining law and order in the event of migration-related demonstrations, including anti-migration protests.

One of the key aspects, therefore, to consider when it comes to the police and migration is the police's professional autonomy with democratic civilian control, the level of professional standards of management, internal control (of the police organization but also among the police personnel), and ensuring that training takes into account challenges of policing immigration, as well as that 'high standards of police ethics, discipline and integrity in public security provision' are in place (DCAF, unknown). To this end, the Council of Europe's 1994 guidelines on 'police training concerning migrants and ethnic relations' compiles practical guidance based on training in several European countries. One of the important points raised is that training alone is not enough to change organizational culture. The benefits of training can be annulled when 'trainees return to the work environment' and are faced with 'negative experiences on the job, pressure from peers, and lack of management commitment' (Council of Europe, 1994: 17). Therefore, organization support, through good internal management, police ethics and staffing should fully integrate these considerations throughout the career of a police officer.

Among the rare documents that consider the links between migration and police forces, one may refer to the 2006 OSCE HSNM recommendations on policing in multi-ethnic societies, which also laid out a number of principles regarding the role of policing for inter-ethnic relations (OSCE, 2006). There is indeed a need to pay attention to the 'race gap' in host societies, whether it concerns transit or definitive migration

> Police ethics, staffing and mode of operation and service provision reflect today's multiracial, multi-cultural society'. (Ibid)

The fact that police mirrors communities at the local level renders it essential. In countries where statistics are available, such as in England and Wales, reports from the Home Affairs Committee found that no force in England and Wales had a Black and Minority Ethnic representation which matched its local demographic (BBC, 2016).[6]

Democratic policing involves effectiveness and accountability. In countries where such democratic conditions are not met, bribery and police abuse are two central issues that negatively impact migrants' journey. Corruption of the police and security sector forces is a more structural issue since research has shown that there is a correlation between countries of emigration and high levels of corruption (Carling, Paasche and Siegel, 2015). Where there is a severe level of corruption, such as in East Timor, Guyana and Sudan, these authors show that emigration is high. On the other hand, Singapore, Luxembourg or Switzerland, where levels of corruption are low, are countries of immigration.

A number of abuses and violence by police forces have been reported widely throughout all countries of origin, transit and destination. Refugees, particularly migrant children and women, are among the most vulnerable groups. Thus, ombudsmen's offices, national human rights commissions, parliamentary commissions, police oversight bodies, researchers and NGOs frequently report police abuses. In her research on gender-based violence against refugees and women, Freedman reports the following from Macedonia:

> One woman recounted the behavior of one of the police officers in a detention centre: 'He tried whatever he could get me alone in a room with him. He used to approach me and whisper to me that I am very beautiful and that he would help me out, that he would personally look into my case.' (Freedman, 2016: 20)

Recommendations on how to overcome these structural problems are made in chapter 6. These involve rethinking training, community policing and professional ethics. Possibly one of the real novelties since 2015 is that the police in Europe have been confronted with dealing with higher numbers of migrants and on the streets of Paris or Calais the police have been asked to remove migrants from their temporary shelters. Some reports, like those of Human Rights Watch, have

---

[6] See the data on the ethnicity in police forces and local population in the UK and England here: https://www.bbc .com/news/uk-34606653.

reported abuse by spraying pepper spray and confiscating the sleeping bags of migrants living on the streets (Human Rights Watch, 2017).

5.3 Intelligence services

Intelligence is the collection of secret information to the benefit of government organizations. Intelligence can be seen from three perspectives: 'a process of gathering and analysing information; an organisation which undertakes the process; and a refined product that is delivered to policy makers' (Hannah, O'Brien and Rathmell, 2005: iii). Yet,

> if not subject to control and oversight, the intelligence sector's unique characteristics – expertise in surveillance, capacity to carry out covert operations, control of sensitive information, and functioning behind a veil of secrecy – may serve to undermine democratic governance and the fundamental rights and liberties of citizens. (Caparini, 2016: 3)

The organization of secret flights during the War on Terror questions whether state security, even in liberal democracies, justifies abuses to gather intelligence information.

Although intelligence services should in general serve the objective of protecting the national interest, the blurring of the internal–external security nexus and the externalization of migration and border policies from liberal democracies to third countries, and in particular from the EU to its neighbourhood, has shown the importance of the diffusion of intelligence standards abroad to support and equip foreign police. Thus, intelligence services since the 2000s have been associated with intelligence policing owing to the blurring of roles and in particular, in the Western Balkans, the European Policy Mission in Bosnia and Herzegovina (EUPM) has for instance been concentrating on training the local police to fight organized crime by setting up an intelligence community in Bosnia (Mounier, 2007: 62–63). The diffusion of these standards, interestingly, has taken place within the European defence mission and led to the gathering of intelligence serving the objectives of the mission determined by police officers, judges and the military.

Beyond intelligence in relation to fighting organized crime, intelligence services can also gather relevant information where there is some suspicion of radicalization or where (ir)regular migrants can be used as proxies by some states to attack democracies or control populations. For instance, there has always been a fear that foreigners, be they legal or illegal migrants or refugees, might be spying for their home countries. Diasporas can be the object of intense pressures for the remote control of emigrated populations in destination countries, from countries with authoritarian governments. Thus, research has shown that diasporas can be instrumentalized to 'mobilize internally, gain hegemony within the diaspora, and marginalize or eliminate internal rivals' and even lead to 'internal repression' (Adamson, 2020).

The detection of threats to national security in relation to migration and asylum may be put in place in relation to suspicions of radicalism and terrorism. In line with securitization theories, the link between migration, refugees and terrorism has been overplayed in recent years by a number of politicians. This has led states such as the US and Sweden to screen asylum seekers for terrorism, leading to an increased securitization of refugees. Thus,

> from 2003–2013, both the US and Sweden added new security checks, databases, and interagency cooperation. One lesson is that in response to perceived security threats, states often add new layers of bureaucracy and technologies, resulting in slower, more burdensome processes. (Micinski, 2018)

Like in any other area, the key to understand the role of intelligence services in relation to migration is related to accountability and oversight. The control of intelligence services varies greatly from country to country. While it is very advanced in Scandinavian countries and Belgium, or even in Germany, parliamentary oversight in France, for instance, only dates back to 2007.

5.4 Border guards

One of the key evolutions affecting the security sector in general during the 'migration crisis' of 2015 was the development of a humanitarian narrative of saving lives. The picture of a Danish police officer playing a game with a young Syrian refugee girl at the German–Danish border[7] has been diffused worldwide and displays a new humanitarian function of border guards. In countries of origin, the behaviour of the security sector is one of the reasons behind migrants' decisions to leave and can worsen the difficult journey of migrants exposed to police violence. In Europe or neighbouring countries, reports of violence are regularly reported and denounced by NGOs. In 2015, in Macedonia, a candidate country for EU accession, Human Rights Watch reported abuse by Macedonian officials; this involved migrants being physically beaten and the systematic detention until July 2015 of asylum seekers and migrants 'including children and pregnant women' in the Gazi Baba detention facility (Human Rights Watch, 2015). In Turkey, border guards killed and injured asylum seekers in 2016 (Human Rights Watch, 2015), and at the borders with Ceuta and Melilla incidents with the Spanish forces are frequently reported by media.

Border guards and other security sector forces have also developed new discourses in relation to their role in rescuing at sea and providing humanitarian functions. This is exemplified by the rapid adoption in 2016 of a new mandate expanding the functions of Frontex to rescue at sea. This humanitarian discourse is being 'used for framing and giving meaning to institutional and operational practices' (Pallister-Wilkins, 2015: 53). This is visible, for instance, in the NAVFORMED mission, a Common Security and Defence Policy mission also known as Operation Sophia, which has developed a communication strategy around the idea of humanitarian work. The operation's mandate is:

> to undertake systematic efforts to identify, capture and dispose of vessels and enabling assets used or suspected of being used by migrant smugglers or traffickers, in order to contribute to wider EU efforts to disrupt the business model of human smuggling and trafficking networks in the Southern Central Mediterranean and prevent the further loss of life at sea. (EEAS, 2016)

Thus, the military mission also has some humanitarian goals of preventing deaths at sea, an issue that started to be tackled after prominent leaders criticized the EU for having contributed to the fact that the Mediterranean is the deadliest stretch of water in the world. The narrative has also evolved towards a partnership with humanitarian actors, since the document also explains that a 'Shared Awareness and De-confliction in the Mediterranean (SHADE MED) seminar' took place in 2017 to improve:

> a better understanding between civilian and military actors involved in the Mediterranean Sea, enhancing mutual interaction and assisting with the development of an overall framework for coordinating different activities and to identify best practices to deal with common security challenges. (EEAS, 2016: 2)

The fifth assembly of this seminar took place in Rome at the Francesco Baracca airbase.[8]

One of the most paradigmatic case studies of the migration crisis is the way EU actors have developed a new discourse regarding rescue at sea and the rapid adoption of the regulation on the

---

[7] https://www.huffingtonpost.com/entry/danish-police-officer-syrian-refugee_us_55f8d9d3e4b0b48f67013caf.

[8] http://www.marina.difesa.it/EN/Conosciamoci/notizie/Pagine/20171128_shade_med.aspx; https://www.operation sophia.eu/shade-med/.

new mandate of Frontex, the European Border and Coast Guard. This case study evidences several paradoxes discussed earlier in the chapter: the choice of depoliticized instruments to respond to the crisis while framing their functions from a humanitarian perspective that brings a renewed legitimacy, based on a more liberal commitment of EU migration and asylum policies, to this policy instrument.

The new humanitarian discourse is being 'used for framing and giving meaning to institutional and operational practices' (Pallister-Wilkins, 2015: 53). This is exemplified by the very rapid adoption in 2016 of a new mandate expanding the functions of Frontex to rescue at sea (European Commission, 2016).

It is within this context that the rapid adoption of the revised mandate of Frontex with the new European Border and Coast Guard Agency is worth analysing more closely. In the light of the rising number of deaths in the Mediterranean Sea, which peaked at 3,771 (IOM, 2016), and the many criticisms levied by the UN special rapporteur on human rights, Francois Crepeau, or even by Pope Francis, Jean-Claude Juncker proposed to transform Frontex into the European Border and Coast Guard Agency (EBCG). The new mandate of the agency was adopted in less than nine months by the European Parliament and the Council, which wanted to move fast on this symbolic piece of legislation. The main concern was to provide the agency with the ability to rescue people at sea, which was not initially in its mandate and proved problematic amid the crisis. A big concern for many years, which had already been at the heart of some of the revisions of Frontex's mandate in 2011, has been that the agency is very dependent on EU Member States, who remain the main gatekeepers, while it has had difficulties in buying its own equipment (although allowed since 2011) (Wolff and Schout, 2013). The existing mechanism to cope with a sudden influx of migrants is the Rapid Border Intervention Teams (RABIT). These teams can be deployed upon the request of a Member State within five days of receiving the request, materializing the operational plan drafted by Frontex. Once launched, 'member states shall make the border guards available for deployment at the request of the Agency, unless they are faced with an exceptional situation substantially affecting the discharge of national tasks' (article 8d Regulation 869/2007). Then the team is deployed in five days and asks border guards deployed under that mission to wear a 'blue armband with the insignia of the EU and the Agency' on their national uniforms (article 6 Regulation 869/2007). But RABITs have in fact been only deployed once, on the Greek–Turkish border in 2010, demonstrating the limitation of deploying common teams acting under a single command.

At the same time, even though the EU is developing a humanitarian border guard function, border guards are confronted with two issues:

> Evidence … shows that restrictive immigration management policies are making the daily work of national border and coast-guard officials less effective, as people are smuggled into the EU, bypassing regular border controls. Progressive disengagement from search and rescue at sea is also problematic. (Carrera, Lannoo, Stan and Vosyliute, 2018: 5)

5.5 Interior ministries

Interior ministries are very much in the driving seat of immigration policy. In Europe, where we find all three categories of countries (origin, transit and destination) owing to the internal freedom of movement in the Schengen area, interior ministries and the development of a justice and home affairs (JHA) policy is central to EU migration policy and its external dimension. In the European Union, the lifting of internal borders to facilitate the freedom of movement in order to improve trade, business and people's mobility led to the conclusion of the Schengen Agreement in 1985,[9] seen as a 'compensatory measure' by ministers of the interior to fight jointly against

---

[9] Initially signed among six countries, the Schengen Agreement has expanded to 26 countries. The UK, Ireland, Bulgaria and Romania are not part of it, while Norway, Iceland and Switzerland are signatory parties.

cross-border crime. The Schengen Agreement put in place a common visa policy among the signatory parties. Common rules on police and judicial cooperation were also put in place, and the JHA policy, which still covers migration, border management and asylum, but also cooperation in police and judicial (civil and criminal) matters, was born. The strengthening of what is now known as the EU's internal security and the Area of Freedom, Security and Justice thus emerged out of a necessity to deepen economic cooperation. The Dublin Convention was adopted in 1991 to stop asylum-shopping, a practice that enabled asylum seekers to apply in several European countries. With the Dublin Convention, the principle of the first country of entry stipulates that asylum seekers need to apply in the EU country where they entered and where their fingerprints are stored in the Eurodac database, established in 2003.

The policy trend is that of a reinforced JHA monopoly over the definition and direction of EU migration and asylum policy. Although this argument is not new and has led to the idea of JHA policies being driven by intensive transgovernmentalism (Lavenex and Wallace, 2005), whereby law enforcement agents and interior and justice ministries' bureaucrats tend to bypass national constraints through the EU as a new venue has remained prominent. During the crisis, and even in spite of the creation of the European Coast and Border Guard (aka Frontex) and the European Asylum Agency, policy 'inertia' with little or 'any reorientation of policy goals or means' (Guiraudon, 2017: 150) has characterized the response of the EU. Policy initiatives have not been very far-reaching, concentrating on the security dimension of migration and less on broadening legal migration channels, for instance. Far from agreeing with those who see strong supranational trends (Niemann and Speyer, 2018), I concur that the 'transnational field of EU border security' is definitely one where its 'stakeholders resist change' (Guiraudon, 2017: 151). Even where new actors have joined the 'circle', the monopoly of JHA actors is not contested. These include diplomatic actors (foreign affairs ministries and the European External Action Service) but also private actors in charge of border security, including biometrics, or managing detention centres.

5.6 Private actors

Private actors play a key role in the SSG/R–migration nexus. The first obvious involvement of private actors is through the securitization and privatization of security over the years. Crossing borders has become a lucrative industrial business, where private security companies and biometric technology generate lots of revenue. Gammeltoft-Hansen and Nyberg Sorensen have well documented the emergence of a migration industry and argued that migration was the object of commercialization: 'migration has become business, big business' (Gammeltoft-Hansen and Nyberg Sorensen, 2013: 2). Private security companies and companies carrying out deportation have made also a business out of migration. Accordingly, in 2013 the 'contracts with private companies to detain immigrants in the United States [were] reported to run a total of $5.1 billion' (Gammeltoft-Hansen and Nyberg Sorensen, 2013: 2).

Transportation companies are also central since they are the ones who may be able to end up transporting undocumented migrants on cargos, ships and airlines. At European level, an EU sanction carrier directive was adopted as early as 2001, harmonizing the sanctions on air, sea and coach carriers and obliging them to return third-country nationals who are refused entry at the border of the EU. The directive imposes financial penalties on transportation companies which are at the minimum 'not less than EUR 3000 or equivalent national currency … for each person carried' (article 4) (Council of the EU, 2001). There is therefore little incentive for these European companies to let migrants go under the radar. Yet, businesses that might end up transporting undocumented migrants might do so unwillingly: 'in some instances, the business simply may be negligent, for instance in the case of a private travel agency issuing cash purchase airline tickets without verifying the purchaser's identity' (Chêne, 2018: 4).

In countries of destination, employers also often do not declare their migrant workers or might also threaten to denounce them or just hold them hostage by keeping their passports, as is the case in many Gulf countries. Human Rights Watch has estimated that 'millions of contract workers from Asia and Africa, including an estimated 2.4 million domestic workers in the Gulf, are subject to a wide range of abuses, including unpaid wages, confiscation of passports, physical abuse, and forced labor' (Human Rights Watch, 2014). The private sector can thus play a quite negative role in various countries in terms of abusing undocumented migrants. In Europe, the Employer Sanctions Directive (Directive 2009/52/EC) prohibits the employment of irregular migrants through fines and sometimes criminal sanctions. In the UK, the Home Office has enforced raids on private-owned businesses that target visible minorities:

> Between July and the end of September 2013, 90 workplaces were raided of which 71 are identifiable by name as Indian, Bengali or Chinese restaurants or takeaways. Sanctions, in the form of raids on workplaces appear, in the UK, to be falling almost entirely on minority ethnic owned businesses. While raids and sanctions seem to target visible minorities, the Home Office website maintains that raids are 'intelligence led'. (Bloch, Kumarappan and McKay, 2014: 134)

While the sanctioning of employers might be a means to curb abuses towards migrants, as rightly discussed by the same authors, these sanctions do not address the broader issues around irregular migration and the fact that the criminalization of migration leads to all sorts of abuses.

One aspect that is often forgotten about the private sector is its added value in integrating migrants at work, for instance. The private sector is also key in rethinking the role of diasporas and remittances. Migration policies and the way they are regulated have been heavily influenced by economic concerns and needs, following the push and pull factor model. The GCM gives quite some space for private actors throughout the document and in providing private sponsorship for visas. These are ways we see to what extent the private sector is involved in migration and where multiple connections are identified in terms of how to rethink its role towards good SSG. Certainly, a socially responsible private sector that pays attention to migrants' and refugees' right should be at the core of any meaningful reform.

5.7 Justice

The justice sector has been defined as 'all the agencies and actors, both state and non-state, involved in the provision, management and oversight of justice'[10] (DCAF, 2015) This includes the judicial system actors that may deal with migrants and refugees such as:

> courts and judges, as well as lawyers, defense and prosecution services, state legal practitioners, bar associations, legal aid bodies and public representation programs, paralegals, court personnel (such as bailiffs and ushers) and military justice systems, as well as alternative dispute resolution mechanisms such as tribunals, mediation services and community-based resolution mechanisms. (DCAF, 2015)

One of the core principles is that a country has a judiciary that is independent from the justice ministry or department, and that it is scrutinized by parliamentary committee and other oversight bodies: 'judicial councils, judicial services and law commissions, as well as independent oversight institutions' (Ibid).

---

[10] DCAF. The Justice Sector, Roles and responsibilities in good security sector governance. SSR Backgrounder. https://www.files.ethz.ch/isn/195679/DCAF_BG_6_The%20Justice%20Sector.11.15.pdf.

General maximum duration of regular procedure (calendar days)	
8	NL
14	CH
33	IT
60	HU, SR
180	AT, BE, BG, CY, ES, FR, GR, IE, MT, NL, PL, TR
—	BE, DE, SE, UK

Table 2: Maximal duration of asylum procedure across countries.

Source: Adapted from ECRE, 2016, which specifies: 'Source: AIDA Country Reports. Switzerland calculates its time limit as 10 working days. The Netherlands provides for a six-month time-limit for its extended asylum procedure'.

Prosecutors and judges have a special role in protecting irregular migrants' and refugees' rights in court, but they are also involved in taking judicial decisions on whether people have violated immigration laws, thus balancing between a human rights approach and respect for national laws, even if these are restrictive. In destination countries with a solid rule of law, various measures have been taken to ease the work of judges such as fast-track processing of offenders who have violated immigration laws. This has been used in the US, where, accordingly, '[i]mmigration cases currently account for approximately 30% of the federal criminal caseload each year, or about 20,000 cases annually' and put the resources and capacities of the US judicial system under strain. This rise in numbers is at the root of the development of fast-track programmes. In addition, they 'were also an attempt to reduce judicial discretion (i.e., fewer downward departures), increase prosecutorial discretion, and equalize sentence lengths across jurisdictions' (Tillyer and Hartley, 2016: 1626). In the US as well, Operation Streamline was launched in 2005 in Texas to have a 'zero tolerance' policy and to launch the federal criminal prosecution of people who would have crossed the border illegally (Carradini et al., 2018). Research has shown that, in fact, prosecuting irregular migrants 'had any effect whatsoever on immigrants' decisions to come to the United States' (Carradini et al., 2018).

The length of legal proceedings and the use of detention are also key in better apprehending the role of the judiciary. First, speeding up administrative or legal proceedings in asylum procedure is a challenge as there is a great divergence across countries. As shown by Table 2, in Europe the decision can vary from eight days in the Netherlands to more than 180 days in most of the other EU countries.

Detention policy has also been importantly criticized around the world. In Australia, for instance, asylum seekers who arrive in Australia's territorial waters are sent for detention on Nauru and Papua New Guinea, which is better known as 'offshore detention'. The main issue is that taking the detention outside the country of destination leads to 'an extra-judicial form of incarceration, [since] immigration detention centres are not subject to the same regulatory framework as Australia's prison system, affecting the conditions under which people are held, their length of detention, and their avenues for appeal' (Nethery and Holman, 2016: 1023). This offshoring goes hand in hand with privatization, meaning that private companies are contracting to operate detention centres in foreign countries. In Australia, 'Broadspectrum (formerly Trans-field Services) holds the primary contract with the Department of Immigration for the operation of the centres' (Ibid: 1025), raising questions over whether the private sector is well aware of what SSG means and how accountability and transparency work in that case.

One of the key issues facing the justice sector and migration are the multiple paradoxes existing between laws that increasingly criminalize irregular migrants and those who rescue migrants and the judicial work towards the recognition of migrants and refugees as rights-bearers. Thus there is a clear paradox concerning all countries: while at the international level, and when migrants are accepted within a country legally, their rights are quite well protected, most rights of migrants, refugees and IDPs are ignored in other situations, especially if considered to be 'migrants in transit', or being exposed to conflict situations and even post-conflict reconstruction. The criminalization of migration and the strengthening of border controls, as well as of human trafficking and smuggling, has had the consequence of rendering the journeys of migrants and refugees longer and riskier. Thus, a study has shown that the adoption of Law No. 2015-036 in Niger against human smuggling has led to a change of routes to 'many unofficial ones' in order to avoid 'entering Agadez'. One consequence highlighted by the authors is that 'the trip became increasingly risky or even deadly for migrants. Figures from the International Organization for Migration (IOM) show that the number of deaths in the Nigerian desert has risen since Law No. 2015-036 began being enforced' (Molenaar, Tubiana and Warin, 2018: 17). One could argue the same in the Mediterranean. In spite of the many operations to rescue migrants at sea (the Mare Nostrum operation led by Italy; the Triton operation led by Frontex), as well as various partnerships established, for instance, with the Libyan coast guard to reduce the number of crossings, the Mediterranean route has actually seen a sharp increase in deaths rates in 2018. Thus, in spite of seeing fewer migrants crossing via the Central Mediterranean route, 'one [person] in 18 of those who crossed to Europe between January and July 2018 went missing. The rate last year was one in 42 of those attempting the crossing' (UNHCR, 2018). Also, in 2018 '300 people have died attempting to reach Spain from North Africa; a third more than 2017. On land, there have been more than 78 recorded deaths of refugees and migrants in Europe or at Europe's borders, compared to 45 during the same period last year' (UNHCR, 2018). The consequences of the criminalization implemented by judicial systems by countries of destination but also by countries of transit is thus patent. And, yet, there is little consideration for the link between the criminalization of migration and its consequences on migratory flows and deaths.

In the field of SSG, transitional justice plays a central role in the reconciliation of communities and in the state-building process. While many see the returning of refugees to their home countries, or IDPs to their home region, as a sign of the end of a conflict, the role of refugee and IDP reintegration in severely disrupted communities is key. In fact, some authors have argued for 'recognizing refugees as rights-bearing actors capable of exercising agency in transitional justice processes' (Purkey, 2016: 2) and that this should be better understood as an indispensable element of reconciliation and peace that would 'increase the legitimacy [of] any transition' (Ibid). The big challenge here is not only to have international law conventions recognizing the rights of migrants, refugees and IDPs but how to legally empower them at the local and/or regional level in order to operate successful post-conflict transitional justice. Empowering potential refugees is of the outmost importance in the future of a country of origin, particularly since refugees who make it to a destination country are likely to be from middle-class backgrounds and be skilled. The refugees left behind are more 'likely to come from economically disadvantaged or socially marginalized backgrounds' (Purkey, 2016: 4). Thus, during the COVID-19 crisis there was a debate over expediting the accreditation of refugee doctors in order to help quickly with fighting the pandemic (Taylor, 2020).

Among the successful examples where refugees have been considered in transitional justice processes, the Timor-Leste Commission for Reception, Truth and Reconciliation has played 'a unique 'reception' function that focused on the reception of refugees from West Timor (Purkey, 2016: 10). The big challenge for these transitional justice systems, whatever form they may take, is to include the participation of refugee groups, and to make sure that this participation is 'meaningful' beyond providing mere testimonies and, for instance, being 'trained to help take the statements of fellow refugees' (Purkey, 2016: 13). Yet, this is not going without challenges as it is possible that the country of origin 'may either lack the political will to engage with refugees or may deliberately exclude them' (Purkey, 2016: 14). Often without proper identity documents, they might not be able to travel. Yet,

> [i]n some instances, States have adopted strategies to specifically reach out to members of the diaspora community either by holding hearings at embassies (Chile, Argentina, Ecuador), using technology (Liberia) or by sending investigators to refugee camps to gather testimony (Guatemala, Liberia, Timor-Leste, Sierra Leone). (Purkey, 2016: 15)

Owing to the risks of instrumentalization of refugees by the state, or simply the risk of seeing some refugee representatives speaking on behalf of individuals who have very different needs and histories, Purkey outlines several strategies that transitional justice should put in place to ensure proper 'legal empowerment' from the start of the process. This might involve:

> legal literacy and awareness-raising (public legal information campaigns, community legal education projects, use of media, community training, train the trainers, etc.). Second are activities that target the provision of services and assistance to meet the legal needs of the relevant groups such as the use of paralegals, alternative dispute resolution mechanisms, legal aid regimes, direct legal counsel, and community legal clinics. Finally, the third type includes law and institutional reform activities, for instance public-interest litigation, advocacy campaigns, administrative advocacy, monitoring and accountability activities, and education or training of government and justice officials. (Purkey, 2016: 20)

Embedding this legal empowerment initiatives, she adds, 'can also help to mitigate some of the risks of ineffective or corrupted participation ... and help to guard against instrumentalization and co-option by powerful actors' (Purkey, 2016: 23). Legal empowerment, however, might be diminished by the difficulties in accessing justice.

Corruption of the judiciary diminishes access to a fair judicial system. It also means that corruption is a 'threat to personal security and a possible contribution in developing migration aspirations' (Merkle, Reinold and Siefel, 2017: 12). Thus, prosecuting criminals, militias or terrorists is key to bringing about a sentiment of personal safety in a country. In Mali, for instance, researches have reported that:

> in many cases individuals suspected of corruption are not always brought before court or adequately sanctioned. Embezzlement of public funds, for instance, is persecuted only in very few cases (US AID, 2014d). At the other extreme, it is reported that there are cases in which people are arrested and brought before court despite being innocent because of mistakes of law enforcement institutions. (Merkle, Reinold and Siefel, 2017: 77)

5.8 Parliaments

Parliamentary oversight is one of the central premises of SSG/R. Parliaments are central in adopting reforms of the security sector and scrutinizing the use of public funding by the security sector. Traditional oversight mechanisms involve parliamentary committees and aim to achieve a high degree of democratic accountability. Not only do parliaments also play a key role in overseeing the functions and missions of security actors; they often have a strong budgetary, legislative and control function that is central in the fight against corruption and in distributing resources adequately. Parliaments also have the function of holding ministries accountable and have a legislative function. Their key SSG function involves enacting and/or amending security sector legislation, controlling the security sector budget expenditures and overseeing the executive (Lilyanova and Blagojevic, 2017: 5). As it stands, most parliamentary committees dealing with SSG will be the committees in charge of security services, defence and internal affairs. Some of these committees

Country	Date	Inquiry type	Name	Website report
Australia	2001	Parliamentary inquiry	Lost Innocents Senate Community Affairs Reference Committee on Child Migration	http://www.aph.gov.au/Parliamentary _Business/Committees/Senate /Community_Affairs/Completed _inquiries/1999-02/child_migrat/report /index
Australia	2005		Report of the Inspections of Baxter Immigration Detention Facility and Port Augusta Residential Housing Project, April 2005	https://www.aph.gov.au/Parliamentary _Business/Committees/House_of _Representatives_Committees?url=mig /baxter/index.htm
Australia	2019	Federal Parliament's Joint Standing Committee on Migration	Report of the Inquiry into Efficacy of Current Regulation of Australian Migration and Education Agents	https://www.aph.gov.au/Parliamentary _Business/Committees/Joint/Migration /Migrationagentregulatio/Report
UK	2018	Joint Select Committee on Human Rights	Immigration Detention: Should There Be Independent Oversight?	https://www.parliament.uk/business /committees/committees-a-z/joint -select/human-rights-committee /news-parliament-2017/immigration -detention-evidence-17-19/
UK	2018	Home Affairs Committee	Windrush Children Inquiry	https://www.parliament.uk/business /committees/committees-a-z/commons -select/home-affairs-committee/inquiries /parliament-2017/windrush-children -inquiry-17-19/

Table 3: Parliaments' inquiries over migration and asylum.

do cover immigration policy, which is dealt by ministries of home affairs or the interior. This is also the case for the Civil Liberties, Justice and Home Affairs Committee of the European Parliament, also known as the LIBE Committee, thus giving a strong 'security' flavour to the governance of migration. Parliaments may use different committee systems and can, for instance, launch their own investigations in the event of abuse or incidents but also use joint committees, which might be appropriate in the case of the SSG–migration nexus. Table 3 lists examples of parliaments' inquiries over migration and asylum.

Reinforcing the capacities of these bodies and their independence in scrutinizing similar enquiries in countries of origin and destination, while reinforcing their role in countries of destination, is an obvious step towards better SSG that is mindful of migration and refugees. In countries like Turkey that are considered by the EU to be 'safe third countries', one may wonder what type of independence the Turkish parliament has enabling it to conduct oversight and scrutiny of migration, border and asylum policies. EU external cooperation with third countries should be accompanied by the condition to strengthen parliaments and their committees, their capacities and their ability to conduct such inquiries.

At the EU level, there is also the complex issue of the development of trust funds to manage migration. As demonstrated by Table 4, these funds have blossomed since 2014. They have the peculiarity of being established outside the EU budget, and therefore outside the full financial scrutiny of the European Parliament, although it is associated as an observer. These funds have been increasingly adopted by the EU and its Member States as they provide more flexibility to respond to (post-)emergency situations.

Name	Date	Amount	Objectives
EU Trust Fund Syrian Crisis (Madad Trust Fund)	December 2014	€1.5billion	'The main objectives of the EU Trust Fund are to foster more self-reliance of refugees, helping them *thrive, not just survive*, while at the same time assisting the countries and communities hosting them.' 'It addresses early recovery, as well as resilience and self-reliance needs of refugees and IDPs, in a manner that also benefits local communities, and preserves the stability of neighbouring countries. It supports countries hosting refugees by investing in health and education, economic development, job creation and integration into labour markets, for both local communities and refugees, especially vulnerable groups such as women and youth.'[11]
EU Trust Fund for Africa (Sahel and Lake Chad, Horn of Africa and North Africa)	November 2015	€4.1 billion	• Strengthening resilience for improved food and nutrition security, in particular for the most vulnerable, as well as refugees and IDPs. • Improving migration governance and management, including addressing the drivers of irregular migration, effective return, readmission and reintegration, international protection and asylum, legal migration and mobility, and enhancing synergies between migration and development. • Supporting improvements in overall governance, in particular by promoting conflict prevention, addressing human rights abuses and enforcing the rule of law.

Table 4: List of active trust funds with migration and asylum implications.

These funds, unfortunately, have come with some trade-offs in terms of parliamentary account-ability, in the name of flexibility, visibility of EU action and speedy response to emergency situations. These trust funds are established between the European Commission and donors, which are usually Member States but can also be 'non-EU countries, private companies, foundations or even individuals' (Carrera et al., 2018: 29). They are governed strategically by a Trust Fund Board made from the EU Commission and donors and piloted for operational implementation by an operational committee. Although the European Parliament has been invited to join the board meetings, it has not been able to 'proactively' attend these meetings (Carrera et al., 2018: 39). Where these trust funds are based on the European Development Fund Regulation, there is limited opportunities for the European Parliament to exert accountability.

5.9 Independent oversight bodies

In SSG/R, independent oversight bodies 'include national human rights commissions, ombudsman institutions, public defenders, anti-corruption agencies and auditors general' (DCAF, 2019). Here I concentrate primarily on the role of ombudsmen and the role they play in scrutinizing the work of law enforcement and ensuring that the rights of migrants and asylum seekers are being

---

[11] Source https://ec.europa.eu/trustfund-syria-region/content/our-mission_en.

enforced. This institution, originating in its most modern understanding from Sweden but having roots in China or the Roman Empire with public officers created to check the proper administration of local provinces, has the contemporary function of investigating cases of maladministration by state authorities and violation of rights. Although ombudsmen can be found in the private sector and understood as a mediating function, we concentrate here on the concept of national ombudsman institutions as gathered in the International Ombudsman Institute (IOI).[12] Although these institutions might often resonate more in the minds of citizens who can address complaints to them, they are increasingly playing a role in making sure that state institutions, including all actors involved in security sector governance, pay attention to the role of immigrants, refugees and asylum seekers.

In Europe, their role has become particularly crucial given the rise of populism, xenophobia, anti-Semitism and anti-Muslim hatred. In a 2017 meeting the IOI expressed its concerns on these issues including towards migrants and refugees as follows:

> Restrictions on human rights and fundamental freedoms occurring in some European countries based on threats to security and public order; threats which, despite their gravity, cannot undermine the democratic rule of law in our societies or European standards of human rights. The rhetoric against migrants and refugees, as well as against minorities; rhetoric which goes beyond the right to freedom of expression and can be classed as hate speech because of its xenophobic, racist and Islamophobic nature. The obstacles facing refugees at serious risk of suffering human rights violations when arriving in many European countries. Such obstacles condemn these refugees to subhuman living conditions unworthy of a twenty-first century Europe and run counter to humanitarian initiatives that express the value of solidarity in European civil society. (IOI, 2017)

They particularly highlighted the need 'for a cooperative network of Ombudsman institutions at a European and global level to deal with the common challenges of defending rights and freedoms, and particularly in protecting the rights of migrants and refugees in countries of origin, transit and destiny' (IOI, 2017). This exchange of best practices and pragmatic cooperation is at the core of the international cooperation of ombudsmen. Thus, the Netherlands has established international cooperation with countries like Indonesia and Jordan.[13] The Netherlands also cooperates closely with Greece, where migration and refugees have become a central part of the Greek ombudsman's institution.

Migrants and refugees present a special kind of challenge for these institutions since they are 'vulnerable' and because of the 'political sensitivity' of the issue in most of countries concerned when it comes to migration. They also have very little means to know their rights, they might be too scared to file a complaint and they often do not know about the ombudsman. Also, when it concerns returnees, namely people who are refused asylum or have been caught irregularly and are sent back to a transit country or their home countries, there is very little time even to file a complaint as the returnee might already be in their country by the time they are able to do so. What is also very important is to pay attention to the digitalization of migrants' and refugees' data and how can migrants and refugees also gain data privacy rights.

This is why national ombudsmen need to take a 'hands-on' approach that is pragmatic and brings them to meet as much as possible with the security sector on the ground. For instance, 'the Immigration and Naturalisation Dutch Service (IND) was ten years ago on our top lists of

---

12   See also the International Ombudsman Institute www.theioi.org.
13   The information regarding the Netherlands is based on an interview with Petra van Dorst, investigator at the office of the Dutch National Ombudsman. Interview conducted in The Hague on 20 March 2019. Interview A.

complaints regarding delays etc.'[14] But, thanks to a lot of training and workshops, this has now improved considerably. Similarly, this pragmatic cooperation drives international cooperation. In case of the cooperation between the Dutch and Greek ombudsmen, it is about learning from each other. In the case of migration, the Dutch ombudsman 'go[es] to the Greek Islands' and has accompanied the Greek ombudsman on its mission to oversee the good conduct of return flights to Turkey. Accordingly, 'the Greek[s] are very effective, and they know how to monitor these flights. And people listen to them'.[15]

Indeed, in the context of the EU–Turkey statement, often known as the 'deal' of 18 March 2016, the Greek ombudsman has denounced the derogation from the legal framework that this 'deal' instituted, explaining in a 2017 report that:

> more than a year after the Statement, there is still no integrated management plan, with a clear, stated and coherent narrative, with milestones and deliverables, targets and time frames of implementation that are complied with. Instead, the Greek administration is still operating in a state of emergency, which results in ad hoc arrangements and allows procedures, especially as regards the selection of contractors for services and goods, in derogation from the applicable institutional framework. (Greek Ombudsman, 2017: 9)

The report highlighted a lot of dysfunctional issues regarding administrative issues. At the level of the 'hotspots', it identified a 'low level of expertise in many involved agencies', 'zero control and accountability [notably] regarding open accommodation centers', 'lack of planning' and an 'exceptionally low capability of response and adaptation' (Greek Ombudsman, 2017: 81) and core issues as to the use of the funds made available by the EU and international bodies 'for the management of the entry and stay of those refugees/migrants who entered from spring 2015 onwards' (Greek Ombudsman, 2017: 83). The protection of unaccompanied minors was deemed problematic, as was their integration in educational systems of the host countries. In general, the Greek ombudsman identified two core issues that led to these problems: 'the absence of 'clear rules and implementation criteria' and 'the distance between the provision and the implementation of the legislation'. What is indeed key to ombudsman institutions is that they monitor not only how maladministration might be wrongly implementing legislation but also what behaviour of administrative institutions is good or bad. These reports are public as they are written in English, exposing to the world the state of maladministration.

One may ask: to what extent is it possible that ombudsman institutions improve the situation of refugees and migrants? In general, these institutions rely on networks of other state agencies and even on civil society actors that transmit their message. In the case of the Dutch ombudsman, they go more and more onto the ground to meet the Koninlijke Marechaussee (the military police) or the immigration services. When a refugee centre was opened in Ter Apel, close to Groningen, they immediately went there to inspect it. In some instances, their reports may/can overturn administrations' decisions (interview A). Similarly, the Australian ombudsman visited the detention centre on Christmas Island, to denounce it as overloaded.[16] This was the case, for instance, regarding the decisions by the Australian Department of Immigration and Citizenship to grant a partner visa after the Commonwealth Ombudsman in Australia published its report.[17]

In most countries, the ombudsman has the option to 'admit complaints and petitions from any person who lives on their territory, national citizens as well as nationals from third countries)' (Tibúrcio, 2018). Therefore, ombudsmen are also open to migrants, refugees, and people living

---

[14] interviewee.
[15] interviewee.
[16] See http://www.theioi.org/ioi-news/current-news/detention-centre-on-christmas-islands-overloaded.
[17] See http://www.theioi.org/ioi-news/current-news/ombudsman-criticises-visa-process.

on the streets. The problem is that, in spite of the openness of the system, these are the most difficult groups to reach and yet the most vulnerable. In a report from the European Network of Ombudsmen, it was reported that complaints from refugees and migrants are usually not high.

> This can be for various reasons: low number of asylum seekers; lack of awareness among migrants; language problems; or general distrust of state institutions. As a result, there is often a need for ombudspersons to be proactive in seeking to help these groups, whether by launching inquiries on their own initiative or by making their service more accessible. (European Ombudsman, 2018: 21)

Therefore, partnerships with civil society, or even the training of the security sector, and state authorities dealing directly with refugees and migrants are key to filtering and helping to reach out to the most vulnerable groups. The most common issues faced by European ombudsmen are the conditions in the reception centres for asylum seekers, such as access to healthcare and their integration in general.

> [I]nadequate asylum interviews and access to legal aid, as well as long waiting times, are also issues faced by many offices. Asylum seekers also face problems with registration, such as when they do not have the necessary documentation or the documents they have are not recognized by the national authorities. In some countries, access to basic public services is linked to individuals' national social security numbers, but asylum seekers do not receive a number in some countries. This means they do not have access to basic services and hampers integration. (European Ombudsman, 2018: 24)

Other key independent oversight institutions include the European Ombudsman at the EU level. Appointed by the European Parliament, it serves the same function for EU institutions through its reports of own initiative but also via European citizens' complaints of cases of maladministration. In the area of EU migration and border policies, the European Border and Coast Guard Agency has attracted some attention from the European Ombudsman on several issues.

The big challenge is, however, where states, in particular countries of origin, do not have independent scrutiny institutions or where, although independent, they are not heard by national institutions. International networks and recognition via the IOI or the UN are key in that respect.

Box 10: Relevant independent oversight bodies in Europe that deal with migration and refugees

- The European Network of National Human Rights Institutions.
- The European Union Agency for Fundamental Rights (FRA).
- The European Commissioner for Human Rights (Council of Europe).
- The European Ombudsman (EU).
- The European Network of Ombudsmen.
- National ombudsman institutions.
- Equality bodies.
- Monitoring bodies under the Committee on the Rights of Persons with Disabilities (UN).
- National preventive mechanisms (Convention against Torture).
- Forced return monitoring mechanisms (under the EU's Return Directive).
- National rapporteurs on trafficking under the EU's Trafficking Directive, article 19.

For instance, in 2010 the UN adopted a resolution on ombudsman institutions that encouraged their creation and their role in good governance in public administrations.[18]

Ombudsman institutions are part of a broader framework of national human rights institutions (NHRIs), acknowledged by UN General Assembly Resolution 48/134 of 20 December 1993. The NHRIs are:

> non-judicial, independent institutions created by states by constitution or law, with the mandate to promote and protect human rights. States are free to decide the best type of NHRI for their domestic purposes. In Europe, the most common models are ombudsman institutions, human rights commissions, hybrid institutions, and human rights institutes and centers. (IOI, 2019)

These institutions played an important role in the negotiations leading to the Global Compacts through a task force established by the Global Alliance of National Human Rights Institutions (Kämpf, 2019: 5) A survey of 32 NHRI across all regions has shown that all institutions are working on migrants' rights or 'planning to do so' (Kämpf, 2019: 5). Among the key challenges faced by NHRIs and how to improve their effectiveness on migrants' rights are:

> exchange among themselves and with other regional and international institutions, and joint monitoring of cross-border situations and cooperation on individual cases. Training on a range of issues was also mentioned, though not as often. Insufficient resources and lack of specialized staff are the main challenges NHRIs are facing. (Kämpf, 2019: 5)

In general, the survey also highlighted that all these institutions, across Africa, the Americas, Asia-Pacific and Europe, were confronted with the difficult combination of (1) a rising anti-immigrant sentiment and (2) 'public policies that frame migrants as security risks and by restrictions on admission to the country placed by governments', severely affecting their work (Kämpf, 2019: 5).

Box 11: NHRIs and the Global Compact for Migration

Objective 11: Manage borders in an integrated, secure and coordinated manner.

Objective 12: Strengthen certainty and predictability in migration procedures for appropriate screening, assessment and referral, with an explicit reference to 'Increase transparency and accessibility of migration procedures by communicating the requirements for entry, admission, stay, work, study or other activities, and introducing technology to simplify application procedures, in order to avoid unnecessary delays and expenses for States and migrants'.

Objective 17: Eliminate all forms of discrimination and promote evidence-based public discourse to shape perceptions of migration.

In Europe, additional bodies that also play an important role in the migration–SSG/R nexus are the forced return monitoring institutions created by article 8 of the EU Return Directive (2008/115/EC). In some countries, like Greece, it is the ombudsman but in others, like in the Netherlands, it is the Inspectorate of Justice and Security. The Fundamental Rights Agency monitors whether these organizations are operational and keeps an up-to-date overview of whether they are effective enough. Overall, since 2014, the situation has improved since in 2014 10 EU

---

[18] See UN resolution of 21.12.2010, available here: http://www.theioi.org/ioi-news/current-news/un-resolution-on-ombudsman-institutions.

Operational
Partially operational
Not operational
n.a.

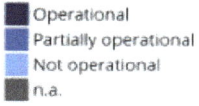

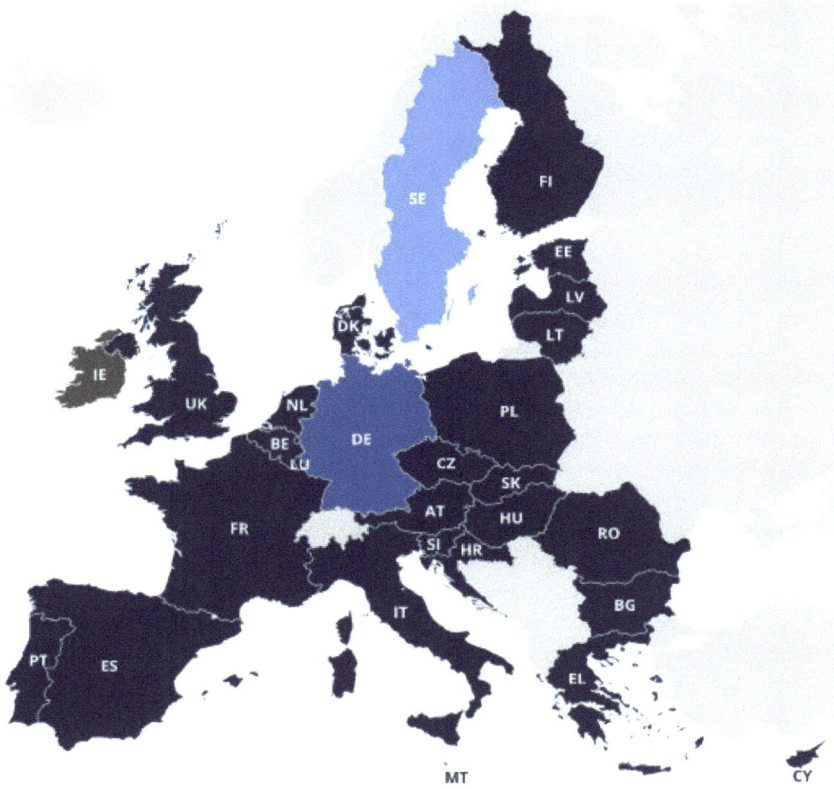

© EuroGeographics for the administrative boundaries © FRA - All rights reserved - Forced return monitoring systems - State of play in EU Member States, 2019 | Year : 2019
Source: FRA, 2020.

Independent system to monitor forced returns in operation

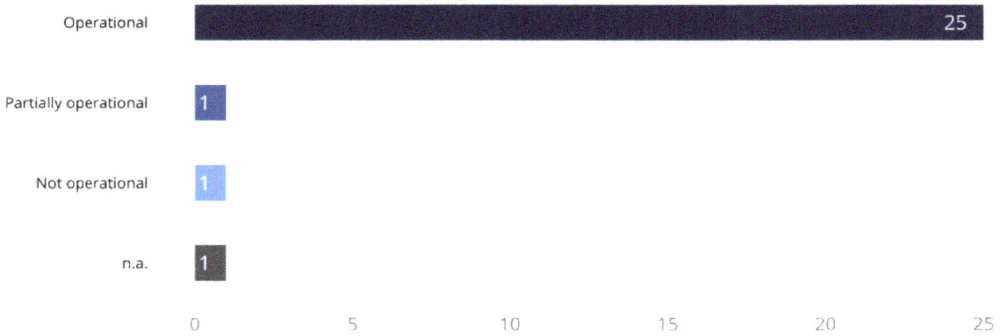

Figure 5: Independent system of forced returns in Europe.

Member States were considered to lack 'operation return monitoring systems' that would be deemed 'sufficiently independent' (Fundamental Rights Agency, 2018).

> By 2017, that number dropped to three – and two of these were taking steps to have effective monitoring systems by 2018. Second, developments have not been linear: in at least two EU Member States – Croatia and Lithuania – monitoring was project-based and was suspended when funding came to an end. In France, the independent authority tasked with forced return monitoring did not carry out any such mission in 2016, resuming them in February 2017. (Ibid)

In Figure 5, elaborated by the FRA, we see that Sweden fails to provide such an independent monitoring mechanism.

5.10   Civil society

The role of civil society, defined as 'as the political space that exists between the individual and the government', namely 'a cross-section of independent citizens who mobilize themselves, voluntarily, around issues of general interest and with a non-profit making aim' (Loada and Moderan, 2015: 3), has considerably evolved over the years and plays a key role in countries of origin, transit and destination. In general, civil society is regarded as playing a central role in SSG/R provided that these organization are non-profit-making, demonstrate independence and integrity, are representative and accountable and show values of transparency and internal governance through financial procedures, recruitment and respect for human rights (Loada and Moderan, 2015: 6). To ensure the highest standards of SSG/R, citizens' and civil society organizations' oversight is key in all the stages of the policy cycle (Loada and Moderan, 2015: 24). For the migration policy cycle, it starts from CSOs' oversight on migration considerations as early as the formulation of security sector policies and reforms, and in developing national migration plans, but also in implementing reforms and delivering services in the area of migration and asylum, as well as in the evaluating policies. In the field of migration, academics, researchers and think tanks are groups that can hold states accountable for their misbehaviour in the field of migration.

In addition, there is a need to pay attention to everyday border practices both by security sector forces and people crossing borders. The way borders are being perceived, imagined and practised determines the behaviour of people and their mobility. Beyond state-led border governance, local populations play an important role on the social construction of borders, and border practices by security forces, which are constantly contested and renegotiated, in particular where there is state failure. The increased role taken by border guards and the security sector in controlling borders and migration has tended to depoliticize the borders. In fact, I argue here that the process of social construction of borders is at odds with the global trend of border governance, which aims at privatizing, externalizing, digitalizing and in a way depoliticizing the border. This 'apparent' depoliticization of the border carries multiple political and social consequences for the ordinary people who cross or are stopped at the border in their everyday lives. Borderlands are also highly political sites of contestation and political mobilization throughout the world.

NGOs and religious institutions, but also trade unions, for instance, are also involved in 'advocacy coalitions' and build alliances 'in defense of immigrants' basic social rights' (Ambrosini and van der Leun, 2015: 104). Civil society is involved in both 'nativist and anti-immigration movements' to more 'altruistic values' (Ambrosini and van der Leun, 2015: 104). To help migrants,

> [f]orms of support offered by civil society commonly target the weakest members of the immigrant population, such as asylum seekers, irregular immigrants, and victims of abuse

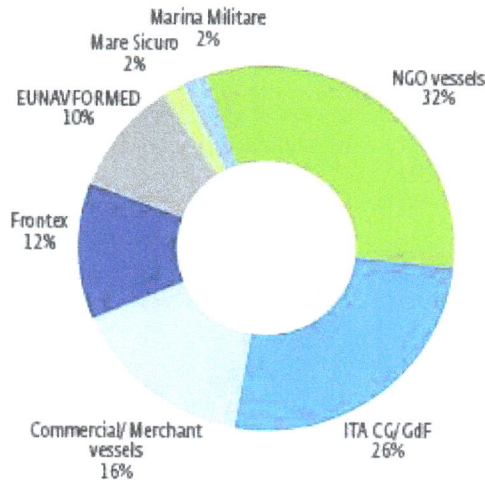

Figure 6: Actors that rescue migrants at sea in the Central Mediterranean.

Source: Frontex Annual Report 2017, share of irregular migrants rescued/apprehended by different entities in the Central Mediterranean.

> and exploitation: categories that to a large extent—with the exception maybe of victims— overlap with the targets of restrictive control policies. (Ibid: 104)

In situations where the state structures are weak, civil society is crucial to respond to migrants' and refugees' needs.

In countries of transit and destination, and at the border of these crossings, civil society has gained a new role in rescuing and assisting migrants. Although civil society at large and NGOs have traditionally been active in Europe to assist the authorities in processing refugee applications and providing assistance to the most vulnerable people, civil society has come to play a new role. In countries of transit and destination, notably in Southern Europe or in the Western Balkans, civil society actors/organizations have become active at the border and have replaced states in rescuing migrants at sea, for instance in the Mediterranean as some states such as Italy are not respecting their international commitments. Confronted with Frontex's lack of competence in rescuing at sea before the change of its mandate in 2016, as well as the end of the Mare Nostrum operation put in place by the Italian navy and air force to rescue increasing flows of migrants between 2013 and 2014, NGOs have endorsed a new role in rescuing migrants at sea. As shown in Figure 6, in 2017, according to data collected by Frontex, NGO vessels rescued more than a third of migrants crossing the Mediterranean. Civil society is thus fundamentally endorsing a new role of rescuing migrants at sea, which is normally the competency of European border guards. Civil society is becoming part of the security sector, although the security sector and politicians have been accusing NGOs of creating a 'pull-in' effect by rescuing migrants at sea.

Thus, we have had various instances since the summer of 2017, when the Italian minister of the interior, Matteo Salvini, refused to disembark migrants from NGO boats, such as the *Aquarius* from SOS Méditerranée, explaining that his European counterparts were not sharing the 'burden' of hosting and processing asylum applications. In many situations, civil society steps in where states and their agents have withdrawn from providing security, safety and dignity to refugees and migrants. In Europe, NGOs have also endorsed new, more professional roles in their humanitarian work, because of incidents with security forces. For instance, 'riot police were sent by Greece's caretaker government to the [Greek] islands in an attempt to regain control of the situation.

These events triggered the gradual professionalization of humanitarian response on the islands' (Skleparis and Armakolas, 2015: 176).

This new relationship between civil society and border guards in conducting search and rescue (SAR) operations brings new ethical issues. According to Cusumano, this 'entails operational and ethical dilemmas, forcing NGOs to accept uneasy compromises on the principles of neutrality, impartiality and independence that underlie humanitarian action' (Cusumano, 2018: 387). Like in scenarios of conflict, one of the key questions regarding civil society is the extent to which it can continue to play its humanitarian functions independently when it also has to work with and be protected by security measures. Working hand in hand with the security forces is, however, indispensable to continue the humanitarian work. Thus, 'on 17 August 2016, a Libyan coast guard patrol repeatedly fired against and then boarded MSF's Bourbon Argos. As a result of the attack, most of NGOs suspended their activities for almost two weeks, restarting SAR only after devising tighter security protocols' (Cusumano, 2018: 392).

At the same time, civil society can sometimes be at risk of being arrested by police forces if they perform activities that are deemed criminal, even if these are also of a humanitarian nature. The global trend of criminalizing irregular migration means that those who save them or assist them can themselves be subject to judicial proceedings. These 'offences of solidarity', in particular in countries of destination, are importantly affecting the work of civil society and have contributed to the polarization with the security sector. In France, article L622-1 of the Code de l'entrée et du séjour des étrangers et du droit d'asile condemns '[a]ny person who has, by direct or indirect aid, facilitated or attempted to facilitate the entry, circulation or illegal stay of a foreigner in France'. The person risks five years' imprisonment and a fine of 30,000 euros (Legifrance, 2019).

In countries of destination, especially when it comes to labour integration on markets, trade unions have played a key role. For instance, trade unions in countries like Switzerland and Italy have strongly supported pro-regularization programmes throughout the 2000s (Ambrosini and van der Leun, 2015: 108). During the crisis in Greece, though, austerity programmes meant a slow and only very incremental role for civil society, including international NGOs. As reported by Skleparis and Armakolas,

> most international NGOs were not formally registered in Greece, which led to delays in their mobilization. When these organizations arrived on the ground, they faced severe bureaucratic obstacles, such as tight employment and visa regulations, which prevented them from deploying, experienced aid workers. Financial (capital) controls in Greece also hampered their ability initially to mobilize resources. (Skleparis and Armakolas, 2015: 172)

As said earlier, CSOs are particularly active in assisting vulnerable populations such as refugees and migrants, but more specifically when it comes to assisting women and children, who are more severely exposed to smuggling, trafficking and abuses during their journeys from countries of origin to countries of destination. It is therefore crucial to strengthen CSOs in countries of transit where smugglers are central to organizing migrants' journeys towards countries of destination. But, unfortunately, human trafficking is a global issue since, according to the 2017 Global Estimates of Modern Slavery, about 25 million people were in forced labour: 'forced to work under threat or coercion as domestic workers on construction sites, in clandestine factories on farms and fishing boats, in other sectors and in the sex industry' (p. 10). Yet, women and girls are disproportionately affected, and people are often forced to work in exchange for debt. The issue of trafficking affects all countries. For instance, in the EU, which gathers countries of origin, destination and transit, EU citizens are often part of the trafficking process, either as victims or perpetrators. According to the same report, victims are often from poorer parts of Europe (Bakowski, 2014), i.e. Romania and Bulgaria. Nigeria and China were main non-EU countries of victims' origin in 2008–10, but later citizens from Latin America joined this group of victims (Eurostat, 2015).

Citizens' solidarity towards migrants, although criminalized, has been particularly prominent in Ventimille, Italy, and in Calais, France.[19] Local citizens helping out migrants on boats in distress have been trialled in Tunisia. Local fisherman from the coast town of Zarzis in Tunisia were acquitted by Italy after having been put on trial for smuggling (BBC, 2018). At the end of the 2000s, 'the "Mom and Pop" small-scale human smugglers and migrant assistance networks claim to provide individual security and human rights protection for undocumented migrants' (Murphy Erfani, 2007: 43). These types of network have been crucial in providing security to many migrants and should be central to acknowledging the migration–SSG nexus.

Box 12: Civil society and migration

- Civil society and the security sector are increasingly interacting in the same spatial geographies of migration, for instance through search and rescue operations or at borders and crossing points.
- Civil society is undertaking a new role by stepping in where security forces are weak or where the state is reluctant to respect its international commitments, such as in Southern Europe.
- A strong civil society is key to leading advocacy in advancing migrants' and refugees' rights in countries of origin, transit and destination.
- Civil society organizations are being criminalized throughout the world for rescuing migrants at sea, which is a worrying trend.

---

[19] See for instance Zamponi, L. (2018). From border to border: Refugee solidarity activism in Italy across space, time, and practices. In *Solidarity Mobilizations in the 'Refugee Crisis'* (pp. 99–123). Palgrave Macmillan.

CHAPTER 6

Conclusions and Policy Recommendations

Migration is a transnational issue that is multifaceted in terms of the reasons that people leave their country and how they travel. Global typologies of countries of origin, transit and destination are uneasy and reveal how, in spite of the Global Compact of Migration, international migration governance is still very much state-centric. Similarly, categorizing people as migrants, asylum seekers and refugees is also an uneasy process, because of the multiplicity of complex personal situations, with people having started their initial journeys as regular migrants but continuing them under different circumstances and state-centred definitions that might criminalize them. Along those journeys, SSR actors are in constant interaction with people leaving their countries and, depending on the circumstances, might even be one of the reasons why someone want to flee their country.

Conceptualized in the nineties, SSG is also attached to this state-centric dimension, which is inherently challenging given the transnational nature of migration. This is why I am recommending thinking about SSG in a decentred way, namely thinking about SSG as legitimate authority institutions in a way that moves beyond a state-centric dimension. That may involve a subnational, transnational and global dimension. But maybe the most important point is to be able to move away from the central notion of the 'state', which has become the main focus of migration governance. Prioritizing state interests and often the interests of states in the West inhibits apprehending other dimensions that might be more peripheral. For instance, one may consider that cities and therefore SSG actors at the municipal level do play a crucial role in hosting migrants in the urban environment and guaranteeing access to resources. Alternatively, transnational cooperation across the border forces of the so-called 'transit countries' could help in rethinking how SSR can support migrants' journeys and maybe identify some regional dynamics where countries can share their best practices in similar linguistic and cultural settings.

Obviously, ethics is key here. Migration is rarely a choice and therefore migrants, refugees and asylum seekers are clearly vulnerable people. Throughout their journeys they face considerable

How to cite this book chapter:
Wolff, S. 2021. *The Security Sector Governance–Migration Nexus: Rethinking how Security Sector Governance matters for migrants' rights*. Pp. 51–56. London: Ubiquity Press. DOI: https://doi.org/10.5334/bcl.f. License: CC-BY-NC

discrimination. Worse, this paper has shown that some SSR actors might play a triggering role in people leaving their country owing to police violence or abuse, or that SSR actors might also provide additional violence through bribery or maladministration, which impacts migrants' integration in their host societies. Revisiting the ethics of SSR actors is key in that respect.

SSR actors are themselves a solution since they are 'reformers in their own right' (Donais, 2018: 34). Given the complexity of migration, there is also a need to think beyond the short-term needs of a 'train and equip' approach to a pragmatic 'establishment of robust mechanisms guaranteeing accountability, transparency and democratic control' (Donais, 2018: 34). This should be integrated into a 'process-focused' practice of SSG that thinks not only about the means to create SSG but also about 'recasting state building as an iterative, dynamic process of strengthening state–society relations' (OECD, 2011, in Donais, 2018: 40). Then it should be about empowering migrants and refugees at all stages and ensuring their rights and safety. The state-building dimension is of course important, but migration requires a more dynamic vision that goes beyond the nation state structure. Migration and refugees bring transnational challenges that need to be dealt with across different levels of governance. One of the solutions is probably to work around the concept of communities and how both migrants, refugees and IDPs, together with security sector, are part of the process. Thinking about the role that diasporas may play in SSG is also needed.

This mapping of SSG has shown how its actors can play a key role in increasing the safety of migrants, refugees and IDPs. SSG/R, fundamentally by its nature, has a preventive nature in diminishing the hazards met by forcibly displaced people on their journeys, but also in addressing the root causes of migration. If one comes to consider that bad SSG is a source of migration, it is crucial to consider and rethink SSR programmes so that they are understood as a long-term investment in people's safety and to ensure that the lack of safety does not become a root cause of migration. The idea here is to improve coordination between SSG/R and migration experts and to develop more joined-up initiatives and projects. Instead of channelling funding to the SSG/R in various third countries in order to improve border management, a full SSG approach should be integrated in these development aid projects.

6.1 Designing and delivering migration-aware SSG programmes

A first priority is for external donors and recipients to include migration, right from the start, in the design and implementation of SSG programmes, including legal references, training and capacity building **on** migrants' and refugees' international law conventions, but also regional ones, as for instance in the case of ECOWAS. Developing more joined-up initiatives, where migration is mainstreamed to SSG programmes and, vice-versa, where migration programmes include SSG objectives in order to address the root causes of migration, would be welcomed. Consulting migrant and refugee organizations or relevant civil society actors during the design, delivery and evaluation phase seems crucial to understand the specificities of migration in each country or region. Finally, there is in-depth work to raise awareness in training about SSG being not only for the safety of 'citizens' in a state-centric approach but rather for communities and vulnerable people such as migrants and refugees. I propose specific recommendations below for the military, police forces, judicial systems and independent oversight bodies.

6.2 Military

Revisiting together with military actors the risks and dangers that the militarization of border control involves is a first step to initiate self-reflection in armies. As we have discussed, the military function has evolved considerably and also involves some humanitarian functions towards migrants and refugees. Raising awareness and training military personal on the vulnerability of migrants and refugees is key, including human rights and ethical training that should be systematized. In countries of origin, transit and destination, training on providing security to refugees and ensuring their safety should be encouraged. Independent oversight of the military should involve making sure that migrants and refugees, like citizens, can easily access complaint mechanisms and are made aware of those mechanisms. Where the military is in charge of maintaining public order, develop programmes that include relevant training with a strong emphasis on human rights protection and on tactical procedures aimed at preventing the use of force. Finally, national dialogues could be set up to involve the military and how it sees its role vis-à-vis migrants and refugees and what contribution they can make to maintaining national cohesion and unity while protecting citizens and vulnerable populations.

6.3 Police forces

Although there is already agreement on the training of police in performing their core tasks (public order, arrest, detention, protecting human rights, protecting the state security etc.) in a human rights-friendly manner, extra attention should be devoted on how to deal with vulnerable groups such as migrants and refugees in the field of human resources policies and effective accountability mechanisms. As police forces might be the first point of contact for migrants and refugees, raising awareness on their vulnerability and training on how to deal with these populations is key. Several options are possible, such as drawing lessons from community policing, which focuses on building ties with communities and whose principle of decentralization, where citizens are seen as co-partners, could be beneficial to work more in hand with migrants' and refugees' communities. Raising awareness among various stakeholders that police forces are not only there to maintain order but also have a preventive function in local communities could play an important role. In that sense, efforts should strive to make sure that migrants are not being discriminated against in the performance of police forces' role and to fight racism and police brutality, which is an emerging topic. Although that aspect can be strengthened through independent oversight police bodies, it seems an important aspect to tackle in police academies and training. One recommendation could be to include migration issues in the training topic of 'policing vulnerable groups', as well as including good behaviour towards migrants in the personnel performance processes of police agencies and police officers, as training alone is definitely not enough.

6.4 Intelligence services

Intelligence services gather intelligence among migrants and refugee communities including for counter-terrorism or for national security purposes. The 2020 assassination of French teacher Samuel Paty by a Chechen refugee has again relaunched a discussion about radicalization among immigrant and refugee communities. The role of intelligence services in relation to migrants and refugees can in fact play a preventive function, being especially involved in the documentation of migrants', refugees' and asylum seekers' identity in order to ensure the extraction of former combatants, war criminals and other potentially dangerous individuals from the group of migrants and their handover to judicial authorities.

Yet, this role, like for other SSR actors, needs to take place within a strong oversight framework. It is therefore key to strengthen parliamentary oversight and other forms of democratic control of intelligence activities targeting migrants, refugees, asylum seekers and diasporas suspected of posing security threats. The setting up of a legal framework and clear procedures specifying under which conditions and how, and under clearly designed external supervision of formal oversight institutions, is important. Given the extent of the external diffusion of intelligence standards associated with migration in many liberal democracies, good and ethical SSG standards of intelligence oversight should also be exported. For instance, independent oversight bodies for intelligence services should be mandated and routinely scrutinize the cooperation and specifically the exchange of personal data of migrants between intelligence services and domestic agencies (e.g. police services, migration services), as well as with the intelligence services of third countries. The exchange of migrants' personal data between intelligence services and domestic agencies, as well as with the intelligence services of other countries, should be based on the law, necessary and proportionate. Based on these criteria, intelligence services should not be allowed to conduct 'fishing expeditions' (searches without specific defined criteria) into the databases of the migration agencies. Independent oversight bodies should regularly scrutinize the policy and intelligence services' use of asylum seekers as informers.

6.5 Border security services

Border security services, through the guarding of borders, control the mobility of populations and interact frequently with migrants and refugees who want to enter a territory or need to be returned home. During land and sea border patrol operations, incidents can happen that could impact migrants' and refugees' rights. Good practice is to ensure that these patrolling operations have clear incident reporting mechanisms accessible to migrants and refugees. As we have seen in this brief, border security service forces are increasingly working together or sometimes competing with civil society organizations when it comes to rescue operations in the Mediterranean, for instance. An option to consider at national level is to make opinions from independent oversight bodies on border guards' work compulsory.

Border security services in times of pandemic need to be supported and to work with authorities to provide emergency healthcare to migrants. Given the limitations on mobility with the pandemic, border security services are also more likely to have to put in place temporary detention facilities and to be faced with overcrowding in these facilities, which present increased health risks for migrants. The role of border security forces is therefore changing rapidly, especially with the closing of EU external borders and the reintroduction of internal border controls in Europe during lockdowns. Continuing to work across agencies and with CSOs including medical ones is of fundamental importance.

6.6 Interior ministries

As the drivers of migration policy in many countries, interior ministries need to raise awareness about the structural need for including an SSG dimension. Dialogue at domestic level across various departments involved in SSG could be led to self-reflect on how migration policies can be improved by better SSG. Although most of these ministries intend to control and limit immigration, they also have an important role to play in fostering the integration of migrants. As lead institutions for law enforcement, ranging from border guards to penitentiary management, interior ministries have a responsibility to set clear rules for their personnel's behaviour and establishing codes of conduct on integrity and to fight corruption for instance. Migrants' and refugees' rights should be mainstreamed within these types of codes of conduct as well as rules of procedure and management processes.

6.7 Private actors

Private actors are involved in all stages of a migrant's journey, whether it is in providing goods and services to refugees and migrants as telecommunication or transport providers, in rescuing migrants at sea (commercial shipment companies), in managing detention facilities, for instance, on behalf of governments, or in providing employment or education (via training) and participating to their prospect of integration in future host societies. Yet, private actors are still mostly seen as providers of funding in migration programmes and, although being more involved in the global governance of migration via the IOM or the Global Forum on Migration and Development and the World Economic Forum, 'the tendency to engage the private sector primarily as a funder or cofunder remains largely unchanged' (Bisong and Knoll, 2020: 4).

The private sector also tends to be seen as a unified actor in high-level dialogues, when in fact it represents a wide range of interests. From a SSG perspective, there is a tendency to consider private sector actors as providers of services to government and law enforcement. Yet, involving more systematically private actors as co-creators and partners when it comes to reflecting upon legislation and implementation law in the field of migration, border and refugee policies could be a positive step. At the same time, processes should be in place to oversee and sanction private actors wherever they infringe migrants' and refugees' rights in their activities. One particular area of concern is raising awareness among private actors about the risks of trafficking in human beings and corruption and promoting integrity principles too in their interaction with migrants and refugees. Involving them as partners in the various SSG cycles and incentivizing them to share their views could be a way to increase their contribution at domestic, regional and international levels. In particular, the private sector can play a key role in promoting integration of migrants on labour markets, in promoting diversity and inclusion (Bisong and Knoll, 2020: 81).

6.8 Judicial systems[20]

Facilitating access to justice for migrants and refugees seems an obvious, yet still necessary, aspect that SSG programmes ought to strive for. There are a number of steps to be considered. First, many Home Offices contract with the private sector for detention and should in doing so include training on accountability and transparency but also access to justice. Another way is to work towards the separation of immigration enforcement activities and criminal justice processes. A major challenge is to sanction systems of detention that are in breach of migrants' and refugees' rights, which is a key role for judicial actors. The latter also need to enforce the *non-refoulement* principle and protect migrants. Ensuring speedy decisions of legal procedures regarding asylum and residency permits is also a way to protect migrants' rights.

6.9 Parliaments

The role of oversight by parliaments on SSG has always been fundamental and should be strengthened in relation to migration and asylum matters. For instance, access by parliaments and in particular of committees on migration/home affairs to full information, as well as improving their specialized skills and analytical capacity on the migration–SSG nexus, should be systematically encouraged by donors and in SSG programmes. In particular, parliaments should be enabled to exert their oversight functions where there is a suspicion of abuses in relation to migration and to create special investigation commissions. Another important step is to integrate migrants as a cross-cutting issue for all regular oversight activities of parliamentary committees dealing with the security sector (including defence, intelligence and police).

---

[20] Some of these recommendations are inspired by the 'Open letter from the United Nations High Commission for Human Rights on protecting and promoting the human rights of all migrants within the global compact on safe, regular and orderly migration', 16 February 2018.

6.10 Independent oversight bodies

A first step for any SSG is to have independent oversight in place to scrutinize the police, military and border forces in case there is abuse at the border. The multiplication of training and partnerships of institutions in charge of dealing with migrants and refugees on how to offer and make these vulnerable populations aware of complaint mechanisms seems important, together with more on-site visits of detention centres but also at the border by independent oversight bodies. Another option is to make a wider use of own-initiative reports wherever possible to investigate cases, as this has the potential to lead to changes in policy. Structurally, the channelling of aid to develop the institutional capacities of ombudsmen and other independent oversight bodies in countries of origin and transit seems crucial as they are often under-resourced. Finally, the strengthening of domestic and transnational cooperation among agencies that work with migration and refugees (immigration services, interior ministries, security agencies etc.) and independent oversight bodies through regular consultation mechanisms could be another positive step.

6.11 Civil society

CSOs are a key partner in supporting migrants' and refugees' rights and should be involved through consultation and independent expert advice as well as in oversight bodies in all stages of the SSG policy cycle. Awareness should be raised among CSO actors to work more closely and up front in the design of programmes with SSR actors. Tripartite dialogue could be initiated in origin and transit countries between donors, government and civil society organizations in a systematic way before any relevant high-level dialogue on migration or embedded in programmatic oversight, as has been the case for the Tunisian tripartite dialogue instituted between the EU, the Tunisian government and CSOs in the field of gender and migration.

In 2020, the COVID-19 pandemic and the imposition of social distancing measures, as well as a legal environment that increasingly criminalizes help and solidarity towards migrants, have led CSOs to desert the Mediterranean, leaving it mostly to border guards to patrol and rescue migrants at sea. The pandemic did not halt sea crossings and we see that, with the perspective of Brexit, human smugglers are also accelerating Channel sea crossings, in very difficult conditions. Some CSOs' resources have also been shifted from working with migrants in the Mediterranean to supporting Southern European hospitals with the pandemic, as in the case of Médecins Sans Frontières. Although not always possible on the ground, the presence of CSOs in the governance structures of border security services as advisers should continue to be encouraged.

References

Adamson, F. B. (2020). Non-state authoritarianism and diaspora politics. *Global Networks, 20*(1), 150–169.

Ambrosini, M., & Van der Leun, J. (2015). Introduction to the special issue: Implementing human rights: Civil society and migration policies. *Journal of Immigrant & Refugee Studies, 13*(2), 103–115.

Anderson, B. J., & Anderson, B. L. (2000). Doing the dirty work? The global politics of domestic labour. Palgrave Macmillan.

Anderson, B., & Blinder, S. (2017). *Who counts as a migrant? Definitions and their consequences: migration observatory briefing.* The Migration Observatory.

Azam, J. P., & Gubert, F. (2006). Migrants' remittances and the household in Africa: a review of evidence. *Journal of African Economies, 15*(suppl_2), 426–462.

Bakowski, P. (2014). *The problem of human trafficking on the European Union.* European Parliamentary Research Service, Briefing, 09/04/2014.

Baldwin-Edwards, M., & Lutterbeck, D. (2018). Coping with the Libyan migration crisis. *Journal of Ethnic and Migration Studies.* DOI: https://doi.org/10.1080/1369183X.2018.1468391

Bastick, K., & Grimm, K. (2007). *Security sector responses to trafficking in human beings. Democratic control of armed forces.*

BBC. (2016). *Police ethnic diversity record 'shocking', MPs warn.* https://www.bbc.com/news/uk-36348750

BBC. (2018). *Italy acquits Tunisian 'migrant smuggling' fishermen.* https://www.bbc.com/news/world-africa-45613072

Bisong, A., & Knoll, A. (2020). *Mapping private sector engagement along the migration cycle.* https://ecdpm.org/wp-content/uploads/Mapping-Private-Sector-Engagement-Along-Migration-Cycle-Full-Report-ECDPM-March-2020.pdf

Bloch, A., Kumarappan, L., & McKay, S. (2014). Employer sanctions: The impact of workplace raids and fines on undocumented migrants and ethnic enclave employers. *Critical Social Policy, 35*(1), 132–151.

Boswell, C. (2003). The 'external dimension' of EU immigration and asylum policy. *International Affairs, 79*(3), 619–638.

Boucher, A., & Gest, J. (2014). Migration studies at a crossroads: A critique of immigration regime typologies. *Migration Studies, 3*(2), 182–198.

Brekke, J. P., & Brochmann, G. (2015). Stuck in transit: Secondary migration of asylum seekers in Europe, national differences, and the Dublin regulation. *Journal of Refugee Studies, 28*(2), 145–162.

Bryden, A., & Scherrer, V. (Eds.). (2012). *Disarmament, demobilization and reintegration and security sector reform: insights from UN experience in Afghanistan, Burundi, the Central African Republic and the Democratic Republic of the Congo*. Lit.

Caparini, M. (2016). Controlling and overseeing intelligence services in democratic states. In *Democratic Control of Intelligence Services*. Routledge, 25–46.

Carling, J. (2016). *The end of migrants as we know them?* UNU-MERIT United Nations University. bit.ly/endofmigrants.

Carling, J., Paasche, E., & Siegel, M. (2015). *Finding connections: the nexus between migration and corruption*. Migration Policy. https://www.migrationpolicy.org/article /finding-connections-nexus-between-migration-and-corruption

Carradini, M., Kringen, J. A., Simich, L., Berberich, K., & Emigh, M. (2018). *Operation Streamline: No evidence that criminal prosecution deters migration*. https://www.immigrationresearch.org /system/files/Operation_Streamline.pdf

Carrera, S. et al. (2018). *Oversight and management of the EU trust funds democratic account-ability challenges and promising practices*. Study commissioned by the Directorate General for Internal Policies, Policy Department D: Budgetary Affairs, European Parliament, 14 May, PE 603.821.

Carrera, S., Lannoo, K., Stefan, M., & Vosyliute, L. (2015). *Some EU governments leaving the UN Global Compact on Migration: A contradiction in terms?* CEPS Policy Insights, No 2018/15, November 2018.

Causes of Migration and Forced Displacement. Deutsche Gesellschaft fur Internationale Zusammenarbeit (GIZ) GmbH.

Cerruti, M. (2020, 13 March). *5 salient facts about intra-regional migration in South America*. Migration Data Portal. https://migrationdataportal.org/blog/5-rasgos-destacados-de-la -migracion-intra-regional-en-america-del-sur

Chêne, M. (2018). *Corruption at borders*. U4 Expert Answer, Anti-Corruption Center. https:// knowledgehub.transparency.org/helpdesk/corruption-at-the-border

Chetail, V., & Braeunlich, M. A. (2013). *Stranded migrants: Giving structure to a multifaceted notion*. Global Migration Research Papers, No. 5/2013 (December 2013), pp. 4–5. http://bit .ly/12Ksm3Q

Clandestino (2019). *Definitions*. Database on Irregular Migration. http://irregular-migration.net /index.php?id=157

Collett, E., & Ahad, A. (2017). EU migration partnerships: A work in progress. Working Paper, MPI Europe. Accessed October 1, 2020. https://www.migrationpolicy.org/research /eu-migration-partnerships-work-progress

Collyer, M., & de Haas, H. (2012). Developing dynamic categorisations of transit migration. *Population Space and Place, 18*, 468–481.

Council of the EU. (2001). Directive 2001/51/EC of 28 June 2001 supplementing the provisions of article 26 of the Convention implementing the Schengen Agreement of 14 June 1985.

Cusumano, E. (2018). The sea as humanitarian space: Non-governmental search and rescue dilemmas on the Central Mediterranean migratory route. *Mediterranean Politics, 23*(3), 387–394.

Davies, T., Isakjee, A., & Dhesi, S. (2017). Violent inaction: The necropolitical experience of refugees in Europe. *Antipode, 49*(5), 1263–1284.

DCAF. (2015). Security sector governance. Applying the principles of good governance to the security sector. SSR Backgrounder. DCAF.

DCAF. (2018). *SSR overview*. https://issat.dcaf.ch/Learn/SSR-Overview

DCAF. (2019). *Independent oversight*. https://www.dcaf.ch/independent-oversight

DCAF. (unknown). *The police. Roles and responsibilities in good security sector governance*. http://ssrbackgrounders.org/fall.php?p=16&l=EN

Deng, F. M. (2004). The impact of state failure on migration. *Mediterranean Quarterly, 15*(4), 16–36.

Devillard, A., Bacchi, A., & Noack, M. (2015). *A survey on migration policies in West Africa*. ICMPD and IOM.

Donais, T. (2018). Security sector reform and the challenge of vertical integration. *Journal of Intervention and Statebuilding, 12*(1), 31–47.

Düvell, F. (2012). Transit migration: A blurred and politicised concept. *Population Space and Place, 18*, 415–427.

Eaton, J. (2018, 26 December). *Border Patrol denies responsibility for death of migrant child in its custody*. https://thinkprogress.org/border-patrol-denies-responsibility-for-death-of-migrant-child-in-its-custody-6200863eaf40/

ECRE. (2016). *The length of asylum procedures in Europe*. https://www.ecre.org/wp-content/uploads/2016/10/AIDA-Brief-DurationProcedures.pdf

EEAS. (2016). *European Union Naval Force-Mediterranean Operation Sophia*. https://eeas.europa.eu/sites/eeas/files/factsheet_eunavfor_med_en_0.pdf

England, M. (2012). *Linkages between justice-sensitive security sector reform and displacement. Examples of police and justice reform from Liberia and Kosovo*. Transitional Justice and Displacement Project. Brookings-LSE.

Eurostat. (2015). *Trafficking in human beings*. Publications Office of the European Union.

Favell, A. (2014). The fourth freedom: Theories of migration and mobilities in 'neo-liberal' Europe. *European Journal of Social Theory, 17*(3), 275–289.

Ferrer-Gallardo, X., & Albet-Mas, A. (2016). EU-limboscapes: Ceuta and the proliferation of migrant detention spaces across the European Union. *European Urban and Regional Studies, 23*(3), 527–530.

Fiddian-Qasmiyeh, E. (2014). *The ideal refugees: Gender, Islam, and the Sahrawi politics of survival*. Syracuse University Press.

Freedman, J. (2016). Sexual and gender-based violence against refugee women: A hidden aspect of the refugee 'crisis'. *Reproductive Health Matters, 24*(47), 18–26.

Fundamental Rights Agency. (2018). *Forced return monitoring systems*. https://fra.europa.eu/en/theme/asylum-migration-borders/forced-return

Gammeltoft-Hansen, T., & Nyberg Sorensen, N. (2013). *The migration industry and the commercialization of international migration*. Routledge.

Gineste, C., & Savun, B. (2019). Introducing POSVAR: A dataset on refugee-related violence. *Journal of Peace Research*, 0022343318811440.

Gómez-Mera, L. (2017). *The global governance of trafficking in persons: Toward a transnational regime complex*. Routledge.

Gordon, E. (2014). Security sector reform, local ownership and community engagement. *Stability: International Journal of Security & Development, 3*(1), 25, 1–18.

Guiraudon, V. (2017). The 2015 refugee crisis was not a turning point: Explaining policy inertia in EU border control. *European Political Science, 17*(1), 1–10.

Hänggi, H. (2009). Security sector reform. *Post-Conflict Peacebuilding: A Lexicon*, 1–2.

Hannah, G., O'Brien, K., & Rathmell, A. (2005). *Intelligence and security legislation for security sector reform*. RAND.

Himmerich, J. (2018). *A 'hybrid threat'? European militaries and migration.* Dahrendorf Forum IV, Working Paper No. 02, 25 April 2018.

Hollifield, J. F. (2006). The emerging migration state. *The International Migration Review, 38*(3), 885–912.

Human Rights Watch. (2014). *Gulf countries: Increase migrant worker protection gulf, Asian Labor Ministers at 3rd Abu Dhabi Dialogue.* https://www.hrw.org/news/2014/11/23/gulf -countries-increase-migrant-worker-protection

Human Rights Watch. (2015, 21 September). *As though we are not human beings. Police brutality against migrants and asylum seekers in Macedonia.* https://www.hrw.org/report/2015/09/21 /though-we-are-not-human-beings/police-brutality-against-migrants-and-asylum

Human Rights Watch. (2017). *Like living in Hell.* https://www.hrw.org/report/2017/07/26 /living-hell/police-abuses-against-child-and-adult-migrants-calais

Idler, A. (2018). Preventing conflict upstream: Impunity and illicit governance across Colombia's borders. *Defence Studies, 18*(1), 58–75.

Ilcan, S., & Rygiel, K. (2015). 'Resiliency humanitarianism': Responsibilizing refugees through humanitarian emergency governance in the camp. *International Political Sociology, 9*(4), 333–351.

IOI. (2017). *Human rights challenges in Europe ii: populism? Regression of Rights and the role of the ombudsman Final statement.* http://www.theioi.org/ioi-news/current-news/human-rights -symposium-held-in-barcelona

IOI. (2019). *EUROPE | Paris Principles at 25: Strong national human rights institutions needed more than ever.* http://www.theioi.org/ioi-news/current-news/paris-principles-at-25-strong -national-human-rights-institutions-needed-more-than-ever

IOM. (2011). *Glossary on migration* (2nd ed.).

IOM. (2019). *Glossary on migration,* IML Series No. 34

IOM. (2016, 1 May). *IOM counts 3,771 migrant fatalities in Mediterranean in 2015* Press release. https://www.iom.int/news/iom-counts-3771-migrant-fatalities-mediterranean-2015

IOM. (2018). Migration Data Portal. https://migrationdataportal.org/?t=2017&i=stock_abs _&cm49=702

IOM. (2019). *Who is a migrant?* https://www.iom.int/who-is-a-migrant

Jureidini, R., & Moukarbel, N. (2004). Female Sri Lankan domestic workers in Lebanon: A case of 'contract slavery'? *Journal of Ethnic and Migration Studies, 30*(4), 581–607.

Kämpf, A. (2019). *National human rights institutions and their work in migrants' human rights. Results of a survey among NHRIs.* German Institute for Human Rights.

Karadag, S. (2020). The moral battle in the Aegean Sea. In El Qadim et al. (Im)moral borders in practice, *Geopolitics,* 12–17. DOI: https://doi.org/10.1080/14650045.2020.1747902

Kirwin, M., & Anderson, J. (2018). *Identifying the factors driving West African migration,* West African Papers, No. 17. OECD Publishing. DOI: https://doi.org/10.1787/eb3b2806-en

Lanneau, G. (2015). *Migration And Development Policies And Strategies In The Ecowas Region: The Role Of Data.* Presentation at Regional workshop on strengthening the collection and use of international migration data for development Dakar, 8–11 September 2015. https:// www.un.org/development/desa/pd/sites/www.un.org.development.desa.pd/files/unpd _ws_201509_presentation_migration_development_lanneau.pdf

Laub, Z. (2016). *Authoritarianism in Eritrea and the migrant crisis. Backgrounder.* Council for Foreign Relations. https://www.cfr.org/backgrounder/authoritarianism-eritrea-and-migrant-crisis

Lavenex, S., & Wallace, W. (2005). Justice and home affairs. In H. Wallace & W. Wallace, *Policy-making in the European Union* (pp. 457–480).

Lawyers Committee for Human Rights. (unknown). *Role of the military in refugee camp security- some reflections from a human rights perspective. Notes for a contribution to the Seminar to*

Examine the Role of the Military in Refugee Camp Security, Enysham Hall, Oxford, 10–12 July. https://www.humanrightsfirst.org/wp-content/uploads/pdf/speech_071001.pdf

Legifrance (2019). Code de l'entree et du séjour des étrangers et du droit d'asile. https://www.legifrance.gouv.fr/affichCode.do?idSectionTA=LEGISCTA000006147789&cidTexte=LEGITEXT000006070158&dateTexte=20091124

Lilyanova, V., & Blagojevic, J. (2017). Western Balkans: Parliamentary oversight of the security sector. Briefing. European Parliamentary Research Service, PE, 603, 895.

Loada, A., & Moderan, O. (2015). Civil society involvement in security sector reform and governance. In O. Moderan (Ed.), *Toolkit for security sector reform and governance in West Africa*. DCAF.

Mamadouh, V. (2015). The geopolitics of EU external relations. *The SAGE Handbook of European Foreign Policy*. Sage.

Mansour, M. E. A. (2015). Population imbalance and immigration as a public policy problem in the United Arab Emirates. In Besharov, S. J. and M. H. Lopez, *Adjusting to a world in motion: Trends in global migration and migration policy* (pp. 308–329). Oxford University Press.

Marfleet, P., & Hanieh, A. (2014). Migration and 'crisis' in the Middle East and North Africa region. In A. Lindley (Ed.), *Crisis and migration: Critical perspectives* (pp. 24–45). Routledge.

Merkle, O., J. Reinold, and M. Siegel. "A Study on the Link between Corruption and the Causes of Migration and Forced Displacement." *GIZ Anti-Corruption and Integrity Programme* (2017).

Micinski, N. (2018). Are you a terrorist? Comparing security screening for Iraqi asylum seekers in the United States and Sweden. *International Migration*. DOI: https://doi.org/10.1111/imig.12448

Mounier, G. (2007). European police missions: from security sector reform to externalization of internal security beyond the borders. *HUMSEC journal 1*(1), 47–64.

Molenaar, F., Tubiana, J., & Warin, C. (2018). Caught in the middle. *A Human Rights and Peace-building Approach to Migration Governance in the Sahel. CRU Report. The Hague: Clingendael.* https://www.clingendael.org/pub/2018/caught-in-the-middle.

Mouthaan, M. (2019). Unpacking domestic preferences in the policy-'receiving' state: The EU's migration cooperation with Senegal and Ghana. *Comparative Migration Studies, 7*(1), 35. DOI: https://doi.org/10.1186/s40878-019-0141-7

Murphy Erfani, J. A. (2007). Whose security? Dilemmas of US border security in the Arizona-Sonora borderlands. In Bruner-Jaill, *Borderlands. Comparing border security in North America and Europe*. University of Ottawa Press.

Nemeth, B. (2018). *How does the migration crisis change the roles of militaries?* https://defenceindepth.co/2018/03/07/how-does-the-migration-crisis-change-the-roles-of-militaries/

Nethery, A., & Holman, R. (2016). Secrecy and human rights abuse in Australia's offshore immigration detention centres. *International Journal of Human Rights, 20*(7), 1018–1038.

Niemann, A., & Speyer, J. (2018). A neofunctionalist perspective on the 'European refugee crisis': The case of the European Border and Coast Guard. *Journal of Common Market Studies, 56*(1), 23–43.

Nyberg Sorensen, N., Hear, N. V., & Engberg-Pedersen, P. (2002). The migration-development nexus evidence and policy options state-of-the-art overview. *International Migration, 40*(5), 3–47.

OECD. (2015). *Responses to the refugee crisis. Corruption and the smuggling of refugees.* OECD. https://www.oecd.org/corruption/Corruption-and-the-smuggling-of-refugees.pdf

OSCE High Commissioner for National Minorities. (2006). *Recommendations on policing in multi-ethnic societies.* https://www.osce.org/hcnm/policing-recommendations?download=true

Pallister-Wilkins, P. (2015). The humanitarian politics of European border policing: Frontex and border police in Evros. *International Political Sociology, 9*(1), 53–69.

Peng, I. (2016). Testing the limits of welfare state changes: The slow-moving immigration policy reform in Japan. *Social Policy and Administration, 50*(2), 278–295.

Purkey, A. L., (2016) Justice, Reconciliation, and Ending Displacement: Legal Empowerment and Refugee Engagement in Transitional Processes, *Refugee Survey Quarterly, 35*(4), 1–25. DOI: https://doi.org/10.1093/rsq/hdw015

Reslow, N., & Vink, M. (2015). Three-level games in EU external migration policy: Negotiating mobility partnerships in West Africa. *Journal of Common Market Studies, 53*(4), 857–874.

Rosecrance, R. N. (1986). *The rise of the trading state: Commerce and conquest in the modern world.* Basic Books.

Silva, A. C., & Massey, D. S. (2015). Violence, networks, and international migration from Colombia. *International Migration, 53*(5), 162–178.

Skleparis, D., & Armakolas, I. (2015) The refugee crisis and the role of NGOs, civil society, and media in Greece. In D. L. Phillips (Ed.), *Balkan human corridor: Essays on the refugee and migrant crisis from scholars and opinion leaders in Southeast Europe* (pp. 171–184). Institute for the Study of Human Rights (ISHR).

Taylor, D. (2020, 25 March). Covid-19: call for fast-track registration of refugee doctors in UK. *The Guardian.* https://www.theguardian.com/world/2020/mar/25/covid-19-call-for-fast-track -registration-of-refugee-doctors-in-uk

Tazzioli, M. (2017). Containment through mobility: Migrants spatial disobediances and the reshaping of control through the hotspot system. *Journal of Ethnic and Migration Studies, 44*(16), 2764–2779.

Tillyer, R., & Hartley, R. (2016). The use and impact of fast-track departures: Exploring prosecu-torial and judicial discretion in federal immigration cases. *Crime and Delinquency, 62*(12), 1624–1647.

Transparency International. (2019). Passport dealers of Europe: Navigating the golden visa market. https://www.transparency.org/news/feature/navigating_european_golden_visas

Triandafyllidou, A. (2020). Decentering the study of migration governance: A radical view. *Geopolitics.* DOI: https://doi.org/10.1080/14650045.2020.1839052

United Nations. (2018). Resolution adopted by the General Assembly on 19 December 2018. General Assembly. Seventy-third session, Agenda items 14 and 119. Available at https://www .un.org/en/ga/search/view_doc.asp?symbol=A/RES/73/195

UNHCR. (1951). Convention and Protocol Relating to the Status of Refugees. https://www.unhcr .org/3b66c2aa10

UNHCR. (2018). *Major increase in Europe's refugee and migrant death rate: UNHCR.* https://news .un.org/en/story/2018/09/1018352

UNHCR. (2019). *Internally displaced people.* https://www.unhcr.org/internally-displaced-people .html

UNHCR. (2019a). *Global trends. Forced displacement in 2018.* https://www.unhcr.org/5d08d7ee7 .pdf

US Department of Homeland Security. (2019). *Annual Flow Report: Refugees and Asylees: 2017.* https://www.dhs.gov/sites/default/files/publications/Refugees_Asylees_2017.pdf

Weisskircher, M., Rone, J., & Mendes, M. (2020). *The only frequent flyers left: Migrant work-ers in the EU in times of COVID-19.* Open Democracy; April 20, 2020. Retrieved from https://www.opendemocracy.net/en/can-europe-make-it/only-frequent-flyers-left-migrant -workers-eu-times-covid-19/

Wingens, M. (2016). Security sector reform: Limitations and prospects of the scholarly debate. *Exchanges: The Warwick Research Journal, 4*(1), 106–119. http://exchanges.warwick.ac.uk /index.php/exchanges/article/view/89

Wolff, S. (2014). The politics of negotiating EU readmission agreements: Insights from Morocco and Turkey. *European Journal of Migration and Law, 16*(1), 69–95.

Wolff, S. (2017). The external dimension of the EU's internal security. In C. Hill, M. Smith, & S. Vanhoonacker, *International relations and the European Union* (3rd ed.). Oxford University Press.

Wolff, S., & Schout, A. (2013). Frontex as agency: More of the same?. *Perspectives on European Politics and Society, 14*(3), 305–324.

World Bank. (2019). *Record high remittances sent globally in 2018*. https://www.worldbank.org/en /news/press-release/2019/04/08/record-high-remittances-sent-globally-in-2018

Yu, L. (2002). *Separating ex-combatants and refugees in Zongo, DRC: peacekeepers and UNHCR's 'ladder of options'*. New Issues in Refugee Research, Working paper No. 60. https://www.unhcr .org/3d57a9ef4.pdf

Zaiotti, R. (2016). *Externalizing migration management: Europe, North America and the spread of 'remote control' practices*. Routledge.

www.ingramcontent.com/pod-product-compliance
Lightning Source LLC
Chambersburg PA
CBHW041430270326
41934CB00021B/3495